SpringerBriefs in Accounting

More information about this series at http://www.springer.com/series/11900

Cristiana Bernardi

Implementing Integrated Reporting

Lessons from the Field

Springer

Cristiana Bernardi
The Open University Business School
The Open University
Milton Keynes, UK

ISSN 2196-7873 ISSN 2196-7881 (electronic)
SpringerBriefs in Accounting
ISBN 978-3-030-11192-2 ISBN 978-3-030-11193-9 (eBook)
https://doi.org/10.1007/978-3-030-11193-9

This Springer imprint is published by the registered company Springer Nature Switzerland AG
The registered company address is: Gewerbestrasse 11, 6330 Cham, Switzerland

Omnia mutantur, nihil interit

Ovid

To my parents, my ultimate role models.

Foreword by Prof. James Guthrie

Cristiana has produced a thoughtful and provocative book on the integrated reporting framework and its journey so far. Also, there are a couple of important case studies which highlight both theoretical and practical consideration for policymakers, corporate reporters, researchers, and students. The book is highly recommended.

Prof. James Guthrie, AM
Distinguished Professor of Accounting
Macquarie Business School
Sydney, Australia

Foreword by Dr. Johannes (John) Dumay

I first met Cristiana Bernardi as a budding Ph.D. student in early 2012. Since that time, we have worked together on several projects and have become friends and co-authors. As a Ph.D. student, I watched her grow and develop her research and writing skills, and this volume is the culmination of those efforts. What makes this book different is its unwavering critical edge on an important topic being integrated reporting. While there are many supporters of integrated reporting, it also has its detractors. However, academic research is not to pit one side against another, but to engage in a critical debate that has the potential to have far-reaching implications for research and practice. This book does just that. It is useful for both academics and practitioners who want to understand the origins of integrated reporting and how it has so far fared in practice, along with relevant challenges for the future. I thus commend this book to all as one of those rare academic works that gives a balanced and critical view of an important topic in accounting and corporate reporting.

Dr. Johannes (John) Dumay, CA, CMBE
Associate Professor of Accounting & Finance
Macquarie Business School
Sydney, Australia

Associate Professor of Accounting & Finance
University of Bologna
Bologna, Italy

Honorary Visiting Professor
Nyenrode Business Universiteit
Breukelen, The Netherlands

Foreword by Prof. Andrew W. Stark

Integrated reporting is a topical issue, with its intended consequence of linking financial and non-financial information and promoting integrated thinking. It has even attracted its own 'standard-setter,' the International Integrated Reporting Council, that has recommended what an 'Integrated Report' should look like and achieve. Nonetheless, although it is mandated for use although it is currently mandated for use only in South Africa and can be seen as compatible with non-financial information reporting requirements in the EU and the UK, its voluntary adoption is at a very low level internationally. Why might this be so? This book provides some insights that should help in answering this question. Having surveyed current academic literature, the book provides two case studies on the voluntary adoption of integrated reporting. By so doing, Cristiana Bernardi provides an important contribution to the general discussion concerning the desirability, or otherwise, of integrated reporting, and the costs (as impediments to its implementation) and benefits compared to other forms of reporting non-financial information.

Prof. Andrew W. Stark
Coutts Professor of Accounting and Finance
Alliance Manchester Business School
University of Manchester
Manchester, UK

Foreword by Prof. Paola Demartini

I met Cristiana as a brilliant Ph.D. student at Roma Tre University.
Since her first research contributions, she has shown great intellectual curiosity for the dynamics underlying the evolution of corporate reporting with particular reference to sustainability and innovation themes.
Hence, her book 'Implementing integrated reporting: Lessons from the field' is the result of a 'research journey' that has developed over several years. The outcome is a manuscript that critically scrutinizes both the theoretical contributions and the case studies analyzed. I highly recommend this book to policymakers, managers, researchers, and students for its depth of analysis, innovativeness, and food for thought.

Prof. Paola Demartini
Full Professor of Accounting
Roma Tre University
Rome, Italy

Member of the Register of Expert
Peer-Reviewers for Italian Scientific Evaluation

Acknowledgements

I would like to express my deepest gratitude to several people, who have shown faith in me since the beginning of my academic career and rendered assistance far beyond the call of duty. First, I would like to thank Prof. John Dumay and Prof. James Guthrie immensely for their unwavering intellectual and moral support over my research journey. Their countless insightful comments and suggestions have inspired much of the enthusiasm that went into the creation of this book. Second, I owe a debt of gratitude to Prof. Andrew Stark for his untiring mentoring and guidance. Our fruitful and friendly conversations have been an invaluable source of motivation in many ways. Third, I am sincerely grateful to Prof. Paola Demartini, my Ph.D. supervisor, for her enduring feedback and punctual advice. Appreciation is due to Mrs. Jemima Moore for her meticulous and brilliant editing work. A wholehearted thank you goes to my entire family and, in particular, to my parents for their ceaseless encouragement, selfless support, and unconditional care and love. And last, but certainly not least, I wish to thank my loving and supportive partner whose levity buoyed me throughout this project. My gratitude to each of the people mentioned is boundless. Without such a team behind me, I doubt I would have been able to achieve what I have.

Contents

Acronyms

<IR>	Integrated Reporting
<IR> Framework	International Integrated Reporting Framework
A4S	The Prince of Wales' Accounting for Sustainability Project
ACCA	Association of Chartered Certified Accountants
BCSD	Business Council for Sustainable Development
CDP	Carbon Disclosure Project
CDLI	Climate Disclosure Leadership Index
CDSB	Climate Disclosure Standards Board
DJSI	Dow Jones Sustainability Index
EITI	Extractive Industries Transparency Index
ESG	Environmental, Social, and Governance
GGFR	Global Gas Flaring Reduction
GRI	Global Reporting Initiative
IAAER	International Association for Accounting Education and Research
IASB	International Accounting Standards Board
IC	Intellectual Capital
IFAC	International Federation of Accountants
IIRC	International Integrated Reporting Council
IoDSA	Institute of Directors in Southern Africa
IPIECA	International Petroleum Industry Environmental Conservation Association
IRCSA	Integrated Reporting Committee of South Africa
JSE	Johannesburg Stock Exchange
MoU	Memorandum of Understanding
SAICA	South African Institute of Chartered Accountants
SASB	Sustainability Accounting Standards Board
SRIs	Socially Responsible Investors
TCFD	Task Force on Climate-related Financial Disclosures
UN Global Compact	United Nations Global Compact

UNSDGs	United Nations Sustainable Development Goals
WBCSD	World Business Council for Sustainable Development
WICI	World Intellectual Capital Initiative

Chapter 1
Integrated Reporting (<IR>): The State of the Art?

Abstract Business is changing. And it's changing fast. The challenges we face in contemporary society are unprecedented and daunting—globalization, climate change, poverty, social inequality, and corruption… to name a few. However, with crisis comes courage, and the voice of the people is growing louder: organisations need to step up and take responsibility for their corporate actions. For some, the cutting edge of this clarion call is what they see as the future of corporate disclosure—Integrated Reporting (<IR>).

1.1 The Roots of <IR>

<IR> is the latest attempt to counter growing criticisms of contemporary financial reporting. In the aftermath of a series of financial crises and corporate scandals, investors and other stakeholders have begun to lose trust in traditional accounting and reporting practices that arguably fail to effectively describe the long-term value creation processes within organisations. The main premise of the argument is that conventional financial statements are short-term, historical, untimely documents and, as such, irrelevant (Adams 2015). Additionally, they do not provide a comprehensive assessment of the intangible assets the company primarily relies on to drive its performance.

Further aggravating the problem is that many stakeholders and investors are also increasingly concerned about how companies behave and report on social and environmental sustainability issues. Within this context, the discrepancy between financial accounting disclosures by firms and the information report users say they need has led to exponential growth in frameworks and vehicles for voluntary disclosures, typically in the form of a stand-alone report.[1] However, these reports have not escaped

[1]The term 'stand-alone' report is used to refer to a range of reports which have numerous labels (e.g., Sustainability Reports, Corporate Social Responsibility Reports, Sustainable Development Reports). The defining characteristics of these reports are that they provide a focus on the environment and/or society.

C. Bernardi, *Implementing Integrated Reporting*, SpringerBriefs in Accounting,
https://doi.org/10.1007/978-3-030-11193-9_1

criticism either. They are accused of being too long, too complex and a sure-fire way to induce information overload (de Villiers et al. 2014, p. 1043). Another critique advanced by scholars is that the non-financial information provided in sustainability reports is disjointed and compartmentalised. If the critical interdependencies between strategy, risk, and the different capitals are not properly identified, report users are far less able to effectively evaluate a company's long-term prospects (Wild and van Staden 2013, p. 6). As a result, corporate disclosures of material financial and non-financial information are falling well short of investor and stakeholder expectations. Enter <IR>, touted as a panacea for all these shortcomings.

Integrated reporting as a concept was first introduced in South Africa in the mid-90s. The emergence of integrated reporting, as developed by the Institute of Directors in Southern Africa (IoDSA), predates the formation of the concept of <IR> as developed by the International Integrated Reporting Council (IIRC), which is the global body responsible for developing the guidelines and practices surrounding <IR>. Formally established in August 2010 as a committee under the aegis of the Prince of Wales' Accounting for Sustainability (A4S) Project and the Global Reporting Initiative (GRI), the IIRC is an international coalition of regulators, investors, companies, standard setters, accounting professionals, and non-government organisations that seek to form a global agreement on a format for corporate reporting that reduces complexity and produces a concise report combining many different reporting strands that demonstrates an organization's ability to create value over time (IIRC 2011, p. 3).

From the outset, the IIRC has taken a strategic path towards creating a globally-accepted framework for <IR>. Beginning with a 2011 Discussion Paper titled 'Towards Integrated Reporting—Communicating value in the 21st century', the IIRC has consistently sought feedback from both businesses and investors on its propositions and recommendations and how practical they are to implement (Reuter and Messner 2015). For instance, the IIRC Pilot Programme (2011) was established as a way for companies to experiment with <IR> and, following this extensive consultation process, the first and long-awaited International <IR> Framework was released in December 2013 (IIRC 2013a). In addition, several initiatives have been launched to assist organisations on their journey towards <IR>. Through these campaigns, the IIRC has entrenched itself as the global authority on integrated reporting and stamped the <IR> brand all over the corporate reporting arena.

1.2 The International Integrated Reporting Council: Stated Objectives and Vision

The IIRC's ambitious long-term objective is to establish integrated reporting and, by association, integrated thinking as norms of mainstream business practice in both the public and private sectors (IIRC 2013a, p. 2). <IR> is defined as "a process founded on integrated thinking that results in a periodic integrated report by an organization about value creation over time and related communications regarding aspects of value creation" (IIRC 2013a, p. 33). The process of <IR> results in an integrated report, which seeks to include financial and non-financial information in the same document to provide an integrated view of how value is created over time and to deliver insights into different aspects of an organization's performance by referring specifically to its strategy and business model.

Arguably, integrated thinking is the central concept that underpins the IIRC's agenda. As highlighted by the IIRC itself, integrated thinking is "the active consideration by an organisation of the relationships between its various operating and functional units and the capitals that the organization uses or affects, [which] leads to integrated decision-making and actions that consider the creation of value over the short, medium and long term" (IIRC 2013a, p. 33). Therefore, integrated thinking takes into account both the critical interdependencies and the trade-offs between the range of capitals that affect an organisation's ability to create value. Namely, the IIRC identifies six categories of capitals, which are distinct but interrelated: financial, manufactured, intellectual, human, social and relationship, and natural capitals (see Fig. 1.1). These capitals can be thought of as "stocks" of value that increase, decrease, or transform through the organisation's activities over time.

The IIRC's stated vision is to align financial capital allocation and corporate reporting with the wider goals of financial stability and sustainability through the cycle of integrated reporting and thinking. Although <IR> started out as an 'accounting for sustainability' framework, it seems to have been captured by the economic interests of stock market capitalism (La Torre et al. 2019a). Emphasis on two of the initial three prongs of "accounting for sustainability"—social and environmental sustainability—has gradually waned over time. In this regard, Stubbs and Higgins

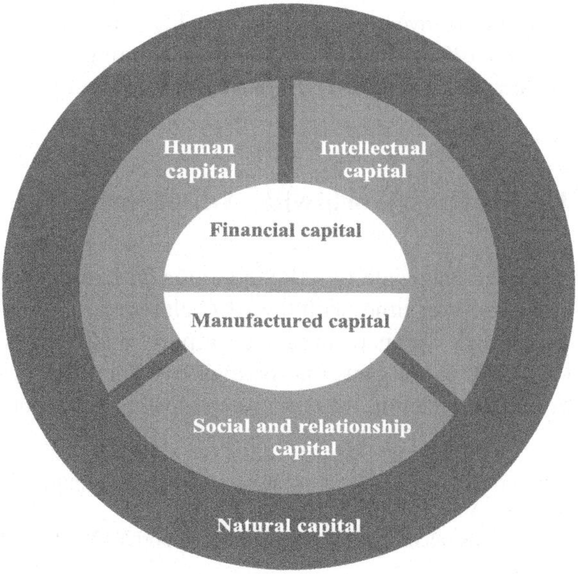

Fig. 1.1 The six categories of capitals identified by the IIRC. Adapted from IIRC's *Capitals: Background Paper for <IR>* (2013b, p. 3)

(2018, p. 489) argue that the IIRC privileges financial value creation over stewardship, reflective of a weak sustainability paradigm underlying <IR>. In the same vein, Flower (2015, p. 1), in his seminal paper, brands <IR> a "failure", asserting that the IIRC has abandoned sustainability accounting in its framework since "the IIRC's concept of value is 'value for investors' and not 'value for society'; … the IIRC places no obligation on firms to report harm inflicted on entities outside the firm (such as the environment) where there is no subsequent impact on the firm."

To achieve its vision, the IIRC advocates for three major shifts in economic governance to help build a more reliable and viable global economy. The first shift is from a "financial capital market system" to an "inclusive capital market system"; the second, from short-term capital markets to long-term sustainable capital markets; and, third, from siloed reporting to holistic disclosure. Behind the move to an inclusive capital market system is the IIRC's claim that "the financial capital market system is insufficient to guard against the multifaceted and interconnected risks of the future"[2] (Labrey 2015). Central to <IR> is the proposition that long-term value no longer exclusively relies on financial performance, but rather it depends on the efficient and productive management of all six capitals; however, traditional accounting methods are only measuring one strand of value. The IIRC also claims that long-term decision-making should be incentivised and rewarded as long-term capital markets are more sustainable than short-term investments. Finally, breaking down the siloed approach to producing reports is crucial for an accurate depiction of how a company creates value, as it challenges management to think holistically, thus keeping current and prospective shareholders informed about the connectivity of the business model, strategy, risks, and performance. In fact, one of the primary objectives of <IR> is to help financial capital providers make well-informed decisions by making organisational value creation stories more intelligible through the depiction of business models (IIRC 2013a, p. 2). However, the IIRC's primary focus on value to investors has been harshly criticized. For example, as argued by Van Bommel (2014, p. 1157), <IR> "risks coming to resemble a local agreement among the few, rather than a legitimate compromise of many".

1.3 <IR>'s Worldwide Adoption

The pace and scale of <IR> adoption in international organisations has gradually increased over time, with the IIRC claiming that more than 1600 companies across 64 countries prepare integrated reports and today's global <IR> networks count over 2000 participants internationally[3]. The <IR> Framework, however, has not yet established itself as the corporate reporting norm notwithstanding the IIRC's vision.

[2]See Labrey (2015), http://integratedreporting.org/news/three-shifts-towards-better-decision-making/. Accessed July 13, 2019.

[3]https://integratedreporting.org/integratedreport2017/index_desktop.html. Accessed November 21, 2019.

Hence, with the aim of both assessing and promoting <IR>'s success, another global consultation process was launched in March 2017 as an opportunity for preparers and other interested parties to identify the enablers, barriers, and incentives to implementing <IR> in practice (IIRC 2017). The follow-up report summarising the feedback and evidence obtained suggests that the main impediments relate to the multiple capitals approach, connectivity, and integrated thinking. Yet, with some exceptions, very little research empirically investigates how or why organisations implement <IR> in a meaningful way.

Despite being a relatively recent phenomenon, <IR> has already achieved worldwide attention at high regulatory and political levels. International accounting and investment bodies, leading multinationals, and the EU Commission routinely discuss and advocate <IR>'s principles. <IR>'s rapid rise to prominence is a testament to its merit and the IIRC's escalating global significance and visibility (Humphrey et al. 2017, p. 31). The growing momentum towards <IR> is also echoed in a number of regulatory initiatives. Although few reforms explicitly endorse the <IR> Framework, many regulatory bodies are cherry-picking some of its relevant features (Simnett and Huggins 2015). The recent EU Directive on non-financial and diversity reporting (Directive 2014/95/EU) is one such regulatory initiative. The EU Directive is perhaps the most significant stepping stone towards fortifying the <IR> Framework's place in common management practice (Dumay et al. 2017). The Directive legislates the disclosure of non-financial and diversity information by certain[4] large companies in Europe, and <IR> is one of the several recommended frameworks for compliance. Additionally, the EU Directive's primary proponent was former European Parliamentarian Richard Howitt, who at the time this book was written had just finished a three-year term as CEO of the IIRC. Therefore, if there was ever a time for <IR> to establish a foothold in Europe, this was its prime opportunity (Monciardini et al. 2016). However, it seems that other frameworks, such as the GRI, which are already used extensively by European companies, will retain their foothold and be used to comply with the EU Directive (Farneti et al. 2018).

The UK has also taken a step closer to <IR> (IIRC News 2018). Mindful of <IR>'s developing profile, the UK Financial Reporting Council has updated its guidelines on strategic reporting, and now encourages businesses to embrace the multiple capitals concept, as promoted by the IIRC, to explain their value creation processes. A growing number of regulatory bodies and stock exchanges around the world have also been strengthening their disclosure requirements with respect to environmental, social, and governance reporting. More than three-quarters of the world's largest 250 companies now provide some form of "non-financial" information in their annual financial reports (KPMG 2017). However, according to KPMG's (2017, p. 24) latest survey, in 2017, only 14% of the world's G250 and N100 reporting companies (both indicators of companies with the highest revenues) labelled their reports as

---

[4]"Large undertakings that are public interest entities (PIEs), that have an average of 500 employees over their financial year and that: (i) issue transferable securities that are admitted to trading on a regulated market in the EU; (ii) are a credit institution (a bank or building society, though not a credit union); (iii) are an insurance undertaking; or, (iv) are designated by a Member State as a PIE (for instance because of its business, size, or the number of its employees)" (p. 6).

being "integrated". Of these, only around two-thirds referenced the <IR> Framework. Notwithstanding the modest global uptake, four countries have experienced a significant increase in integrated reporting: Japan (21%), Brazil (16%), Mexico (16%), and Spain (9%). Thus, <IR> seems to be more accepted in some countries than others (see, Sabelfeld and Dumay 2018).

Overall, these numbers compared to 2015 statistics suggest that <IR> adoption has not significantly grown over the last few years. As of today, <IR> remains voluntary for all firms, even in South Africa, where the concept of integrated reporting was born. Here, companies with a primary listing on the Johannesburg Stock Exchange (JSE) are obliged to produce an integrated report that adheres to specific principles (King reports as discussed later on), but they are only encouraged to use the <IR> Framework to fulfil these obligations (IoDSA 2016).

1.4 <IR> and the Academic Community

With such a fast-growing international debate, <IR> in the academic community was a subject of intense interest from the outset (Milne and Gray 2013) as demonstrated in the special issues dedicated to <IR> and integrated thinking by the *Accounting Auditing and Accountability Journal* in 2014 (de Villiers et al. 2014) and *Meditari Accountancy Research* in 2017 (de Villiers et al. 2017). The articles in these issues represent some of the most highly-cited ones in their period. Further, the special issues continue to come with *Meditari Accountancy Research's* "Exploring Integrated Thinking in action: Theoretical interpretations and evidence from the field" slated for 2020 (Busco et al. 2020) and "Critical Perspectives on Integrated Reporting" in 2022 (Cooper et al. 2020), which arguably suggest that <IR> is, and is likely to continue to be, a topic of debate among academics. This is due to the fact that there is growing discussion about the relevance of <IR> between its detractors (e.g., La Torre et al. 2019b; Dumay et al. 2016; Flower 2015; Thomson 2015; Tweedie and Martinov-Bennie 2015; Stubbs and Higgins 2014; Brown and Dillard 2014; de Villiers et al. 2014) and supporters (e.g., Adams 2015, 2017). Some of the most notable studies contributing to this debate are listed in Table 1.1.

Despite these contributions, the role management control systems play in implementing <IR> remains under-explored (see, Dumay and Dai 2017 for an exception). Most <IR> research focuses on the external dimensions of <IR>, not the internal. Additionally, evidence on the benefits of <IR> and its potential to foster organisational change—and, therefore, its future within corporate reporting—remain elusive. Hence, calls for greater insight into how <IR> is operationalised in practice are on the rise (Dumay et al. 2017; Perego et al. 2016; Adams 2015; Stubbs and Higgins 2014; de Villiers et al. 2014). This book seeks to clarify how <IR>, as a relatively recent phenomenon, is implemented in practice, and to ascertain whether it could ultimately become the international corporate reporting norm as the IIRC ardently advocates.

Table 1.1 Papers on <IR> by area of investigation

Area of investigation	Study
Development and institutionalisation	Rinaldi et al. (2018) Humphrey et al. (2017) Rowbottom and Locke (2016) de Villiers et al. (2016) Adams (2015) de Villiers et al. (2014)
Determinants of adoption	García-Sánchez et al. (2019) Sierra-García et al. (2015) Frías-Aceituno et al. (2014) Frías-Aceituno et al. (2013) García-Sánchez et al. (2013) Jensen and Berg (2012)
Diffusion in emerging markets	Hsiao and Kelly (2018) Gunarathne and Senaratne (2017) Macias and Farfan-Lievano (2017)
Assurance	Maroun (2017) Simnett and Huggins (2015)
Integrated thinking	La Torre et al. (2019b) Feng et al. (2017) Guthrie et al. (2017)
Management control systems (culture)	Binh and de Villiers (2018) Dumay and Dai (2017)
The role of integrated report preparers	McNally and Maroun (2018) Lai et al. (2018) McNally et al. (2017) Chaidali and Jones (2017)
Practical implementation	Mio et al. (2016) Perego et al. (2016) Lodhia (2015)

This exploration begins with a review of the emerging field of <IR>, followed by two detailed case studies on organisations that have embarked on the path towards <IR>. The literature reveals that most previous research has adopted a top-down ostensive stance rather than a critical bottom-up approach as to how <IR> has been implemented. Consequently, the case studies presented here seek to showcase a "soft view" on how two particular organisations have implemented and/or how they prepared themselves to implement <IR> in practice—in other words, the journeys they took to <IR>.

The first case study concerns one division within a high-tech multinational company operating in the aerospace, defence, and security sector, referred to as Omega to preserve anonymity. The second case study is on Eni, an Italian oil and gas company, which has been a prominent innovator in the area of sustainability reporting and a participant in the IIRC's Pilot Programme. Both these cases cast new light on the transition towards integrated thinking and the dynamics through which <IR> might evolve to become established practice. They also demonstrate how <IR> can become part of a wider corporate reporting journey that represents the integration of different reporting frameworks and standards.

References

Adams, C. A. (2015). The international integrated reporting council: A call to action. *Critical Perspectives on Accounting, 27,* 23–28. https://doi.org/10.1016/j.cpa.2014.07.001.

Adams, C. A. (2017). *Understanding integrated reporting: The concise guide to integrated thinking and the future of corporate reporting*. New York: Routledge.

Binh, B., & de Villiers, C. (2018). Management control systems to support sustainability and integrated reporting. In C. de Villiers & W. Maroun (Eds.), *Sustainability accounting and integrated reporting* (pp. 121–148). London: Routledge.

Brown, J., & Dillard, J. (2014). Integrated reporting: On the need for broadening out and opening up. *Accounting, Auditing & Accountability Journal, 27*(7), 1120–1156. https://doi.org/10.1108/AAAJ-04-2013-1313.

Busco, C., Granà, F. & Achilli, G. (2020). Exploring integrated thinking in action: Theoretical interpretations and evidence from the field. *Meditari Accountancy Research.* https://www.emeraldgrouppublishing.com/products/journals/call_for_papers.htm?id=8619.

Chaidali, P., & Jones, M. J. (2017). It's a matter of trust: Exploring the perceptions of Integrated Reporting preparers. *Critical Perspectives on Accounting, 48,* 1–20. https://doi.org/10.1016/j.cpa.2017.08.001.

Cooper, C., Rodrigue, M. & Tregidga, H. (2020). Special issue: Critical perspectives on integrated reporting. *Critical Perspectives on Accounting*.https://www.journals.elsevier.com/critical-perspectives-on-accounting/call-for-papers/special-issue-critical-perspectives-on-integrated-reporting.

de Villiers, C., Hsiao, P.-C. K., & Warren, M. (2017). Developing a conceptual model of influences around integrated reporting, new insights and directions for future research. *Meditari Accountancy Research, 25*(4), 450–460. https://doi.org/10.1108/MEDAR-07-2017-0183.

de Villiers, C., Rinaldi, L., & Unerman, J. (2014). Integrated reporting: Insights, gaps and an agenda for future research. *Accounting, Auditing & Accountability Journal, 27*(7), 1042–1067. https://doi.org/10.1108/AAAJ-06-2014-1736.

de Villiers, C., Venter, E., & Hsiao, P. (2016). Integrated reporting: Background, measurement issues, approaches and an agenda for future research. *Accounting & Finance, 57*(4), 937–959. https://doi.org/10.1111/acfi.12246.

Dumay, J., Bernardi, C., Guthrie, J., & Demartini, P. (2016). Integrated reporting: A structured literature review. *Accounting Forum, 40*(3), 166–185. https://doi.org/10.1016/j.accfor.2016.06.001.

Dumay, J., Bernardi, C., Guthrie, J., & La Torre, M. (2017). Barriers to implementing the international integrated reporting framework: A contemporary academic perspective. *Meditari Accountancy Research, 25*(4), 461–480. https://doi.org/10.1108/MEDAR-05-2017-0150.

Dumay, J., & Dai, T. (2017). Integrated thinking as a cultural control? *Meditari Accountancy Research, 25*(4), 574–604. https://doi.org/10.1108/MEDAR-07-2016-0067.

European Union. (2014). *Directive 2014/95/EU of the European parliament and of the council.* Available at: https://eur-lex.europa.eu/legal-content/EN/TXT/?uri=CELEX%3A32014L0095.

Farneti, F., De Villiers, C., & Dumay, J. (2018). *The EU directive on non-financial and diversity information: A new toothless tiger is born?* Paper presented at the European Accounting Association 41st Annual Congress. Milan Italy, May 30–June 1, 2018.

Feng, T., Cummings, L., & Tweedie, D. (2017). Exploring integrated thinking in integrated reporting—An exploratory study in Australia. *Journal of Intellectual Capital, 18*(2), 330–353. https://doi.org/10.1108/JIC-06-2016-0068.

Flower, J. (2015). The international integrated reporting council: A story of failure. *Critical Perspectives on Accounting, 27,* 1–17. https://doi.org/10.1016/j.cpa.2014.07.002.

Frias-Aceituno, J. V., Rodriguez-Ariza, L., & Garcia-Sanchez, I. M. (2013). The role of the board in the dissemination of integrated corporate social reporting. *Corporate Social Responsibility and Environmental Management, 20*(4), 219–233. https://doi.org/10.1002/csr.1294.

Frias-Aceituno, J., Rodríguez-Ariza, L., & Garcia-Sánchez, I. M. (2014). Explanatory factors of integrated sustainability and financial reporting. *Business Strategy and the Environment, 23*(1), 56–72. https://doi.org/10.1002/bse.1765.

García-Sánchez, I.-M., Martínez-Ferrero, J., & Garcia-Benau, M.-A. (2019). Integrated reporting: The mediating role of the board of directors and investor protection on managerial discretion in munificent environments. *Corporate Social Responsibility and Environmental Management, 26*(1), 29–45. https://doi.org/10.1002/csr.1655.

García-Sánchez, I.-M., Rodríguez-Ariza, L., & Frías-Aceituno, J.-V. (2013). The cultural system and integrated reporting. *International Business Review, 22*(5), 828–838. https://doi.org/10.1016/j.ibusrev.2013.01.007.

Gunarathne, N., & Senaratne, S. (2017). Diffusion of integrated reporting in an emerging South Asian (SAARC) nation. *Managerial Auditing Journal, 32*(4/5), 524–548. https://doi.org/10.1108/MAJ-01-2016-1309.

Guthrie, J., Manes-Rossi, F., & Orelli, R. L. (2017). Integrated reporting and integrated thinking in Italian public sector organisations. *Meditari Accountancy Research, 25*(4), 553–573. https://doi.org/10.1108/MEDAR-06-2017-0155.

Hsiao, P.-C. K., & Kelly, M. (2018). Investment considerations and impressions of integrated reporting: Evidence from Taiwan. *Sustainability Accounting, Management and Policy Journal, 9*(1), 2–28. https://doi.org/10.1108/SAMPJ-10-2016-0072.

Humphrey, C., O'Dwyer, B., & Unerman, J. (2017). Re-theorizing the configuration of organizational fields: The IIRC and the pursuit of 'Enlightened' corporate reporting. *Accounting and Business Research, 47*(1), 30–63. https://doi.org/10.1080/00014788.2016.1198683.

IIRC News. (2018). Available at: http://integratedreporting.org/news/uk-businesses-take-a-step-closer-to-integrated-reporting-as-the-iirc-welcomes-revised-guidance-from-the-uk-financial-reporting-council. July 31, 2018. Accessed August 4, 2019.

Institute of Directors in Southern Africa (IoDSA). (2016). *Report on corporate governance for South Africa* (*King IV*). Johannesburg. Available at: https://www.adams.africa/wp-content/uploads/2016/11/King-IV-Report.pdf. Accessed July 16, 2019.

International Integrated Reporting Committee (IIRC). (2011). Towards integrated reporting. In *Communicating value in the 21st century, international integrated reporting committee*. London. Available at: https://integratedreporting.org/wp-content/uploads/2011/09/IR-Discussion-Paper-2011_spreads.pdf. Accessed June 27, 2019.

International Integrated Reporting Council (IIRC). (2013a). *The international <IR> framework*. London: International Integrated Reporting Council. Available at: http://www.integratedreporting.org/wp-content/uploads/2015/03/13-12-08-THE-INTERNATIONAL-IR-FRAMEWORK-2-1.pdf. Accessed June 24, 2019.

International Integrated Reporting Council (IIRC). (2013b). *Capitals: background paper for <IR>*. Available at: http://integratedreporting.org/wp-content/uploads/2013/03/IR-Background-Paper-Capitals.pdf. Accessed June 15, 2019.

International Integrated Reporting Council (IIRC). (2017). *International <IR> framework implementation feedback: Invitation to comment*. London: International Integrated Reporting Council. Available at: https://integratedreporting.org/invitation-to-comment/. Accessed June 6, 2019.

Jensen, J. C., & Berg, N. (2012). Determinants of traditional sustainability reporting versus integrated reporting. An institutionalist approach. *Business Strategy and the Environment, 21*(5), 299–316. https://doi.org/10.1002/bse.740.

KPMG. (2017). *KPMG survey of corporate responsibility reporting 2017*. Available at: https://home.kpmg/xx/en/home/campaigns/2017/10/survey-of-corporate-responsibility-reporting-2017.html.

La Torre, M., Bernardi, C., Guthrie, J., & Dumay, J. (2019a). Integrated reporting and integrated thinking: Practical challenges. In S. Arvidsson (Ed.), *Challenges in managing sustainable business* (pp. 25–54). Cham: Palgrave Macmillan. https://doi.org/10.1007/978-3-319-93266-8_2.

La Torre, M., Dumay, J., Rea, M. A., & Abhayawansa, S. (2019b). A "journey" toward a safe harbor: The rhetorical process of the international integrated reporting council. *The British Accounting Review*. https://doi.org/10.1016/j.bar.2019.100836.

Labrey, J. (2015). Three shifts towards better decision making. *News*. IIRC, May 26, 2015. Available at: http://integratedreporting.org/news/three-shifts-towards-better-decision-making/. Accessed June 22, 2019.

Lai, A., Melloni, G., & Stacchezzini, R. (2018). Integrated reporting and narrative accountability: The role of preparers. *Accounting, Auditing & Accountability Journal, 31*(5), 1381–1405. https://doi.org/10.1108/AAAJ-08-2016-2674.

Lodhia, S. (2015). Exploring the transition to integrated reporting through a practice lens: An Australian customer owned bank perspective. *Journal of Business Ethics, 129*(3), 585–598. https://doi.org/10.1007/s10551-014-2194-8.

Macias, H. A., & Farfan-Lievano, A. (2017). Integrated reporting as a strategy for firm growth: Multiple case study in Colombia. *Meditari Accountancy Research, 25*(4), 605–628. https://doi.org/10.1108/MEDAR-11-2016-0099.

Maroun, W. (2017). Assuring the integrated report: Insights and recommendations from auditors and preparers. *The British Accounting Review, 49*(3), 329–346. https://doi.org/10.1016/j.bar.2017.03.003.

McNally, M., Cerbone, D., & Maroun, W. (2017). Exploring the challenges of preparing an integrated report. *Meditari Accountancy Research, 25*(4), 481–504. https://doi.org/10.1108/MEDAR-10-2016-0085.

McNally, M. A., & Maroun, W. (2018). It is not always bad news: Illustrating the potential of integrated reporting using a case study in the eco-tourism industry. *Accounting, Auditing & Accountability Journal, 31*(5), 1319–1348. https://doi.org/10.1108/AAAJ-05-2016-2577.

Milne, M. J., & Gray, R. (2013). W(h)ither ecology? The triple bottom line, the global reporting initiative, and corporate sustainability reporting. *Journal of Business Ethics, 118*(1), 13–29. https://doi.org/10.1007/s10551-012-1543-8.

Mio, C., Marco, F., & Pauluzzo, R. (2016). Internal application of IR principles: Generali's internal integrated reporting. *Journal of Cleaner Production, 139,* 204–218. https://doi.org/10.1016/j.jclepro.2016.07.149.

Monciardini, D., Dumay, J., & Biondi, L. (2016). *Integrated reporting and EU law. Competing, converging or complementary regulatory frameworks?* Paper presented at the and EU Law. Competing, Converging or Complementary Regulatory Frameworks?—Life-cycle based management and reporting for sustainable business. Oslo, Norway, November 29–30, 2016.

Perego, P., Kennedy, S., & Whiteman, G. (2016). A lot of icing but little cake? Taking integrated reporting forward. *Journal of Cleaner Production, 136*(Part A), 53–64. https://doi.org/10.1016/j.jclepro.2016.01.106.

Reuter, M., & Messner, M. (2015). Lobbying on the integrated reporting framework. *Accounting, Auditing & Accountability Journal, 28*(3), 365–402. https://doi.org/10.1108/AAAJ-03-2013-1289.

Rinaldi, L., Unerman, J., & de Villiers, C. (2018). Evaluating the integrated reporting journey: Insights, gaps and agendas for future research. *Accounting, Auditing & Accountability Journal, 31*(5), 1294–1318. https://doi.org/10.1108/AAAJ-04-2018-3446.

Rowbottom, N., & Locke, J. (2016). The emergence of <IR>. *Accounting and Business Research, 46*(1), 83–115. https://doi.org/10.1080/00014788.2015.1029867.

Sabelfeld, S., & Dumay, J. (2018). *Adoption of integrated reporting: Lost in local translation?* Paper presented at the Financial Reporting Workshop. University of Bologna, June 14–15, 2018.

Sierra-García, L., Zorio-Grima, A., & García-Benau, M. A. (2015). Stakeholder engagement, corporate social responsibility and integrated reporting: An exploratory study. *Corporate Social Responsibility and Environmental Management, 22*(5), 286–304. https://doi.org/10.1002/csr.1345.

Simnett, R., & Huggins, A. L. (2015). Integrated reporting and assurance: Where can research add value? *Sustainability Accounting, Management and Policy Journal, 6*(1), 29–53. https://doi.org/10.1108/SAMPJ-09-2014-0053.

Stubbs, W., & Higgins, C. (2014). Integrated reporting and internal mechanisms of change. *Accounting, Auditing & Accountability Journal, 27*(7), 1068–1089. https://doi.org/10.1108/AAAJ-03-2013-1279.

Stubbs, W., & Higgins, C. (2018). Stakeholders' perspectives on the role of regulatory reform in integrated reporting. *Journal of Business Ethics, 147*(3), 489–508. https://doi.org/10.1007/s10551-015-2954-0.

Thomson, I. (2015). 'But does sustainability need capitalism or an integrated report' a commentary on 'the international integrated reporting council: A story of failure' by Flower. *J, Critical Perspectives on Accounting, 27,* 18–22. https://doi.org/10.1016/j.cpa.2014.07.003.

Tweedie, D., & Martinov-Bennie, N. (2015). Entitlements and time: Integrated reporting's double-edged agenda. *Social and Environmental Accountability Journal, 35*(1), 49–61. https://doi.org/10.1080/0969160X.2015.1007466.

van Bommel, K. (2014). Towards a legitimate compromise? An exploration of integrated reporting in the Netherlands. *Accounting, Auditing & Accountability Journal, 27*(7), 1157–1189. https://doi.org/10.1108/AAAJ-04-2013-1309.

Wild, S., & van Staden, C. (2013). Integrated reporting: Initial analysis of early reporters—An institutional theory approach. In *The 7th Asia-Pacific Interdisciplinary Research in Accounting (APIRA) Conference*. Kobe, Japan.

Chapter 2
Antecedents of <IR>: Tracing History

Abstract To better understand where <IR> stands today, it is helpful to trace its origins: how it has developed in different jurisdictions, and how it is currently being promoted. The IIRC's strategy was supposed to culminate in what it termed a 'Breakthrough Phase' in 2017. But, as Dumay et al. (2017) point out, <IR> has not yet broken through any major markets beyond South Africa. There is, however, one notable exception in Japan, where a desire to attract Western capital has led to sweeping changes in corporate governance legislation and <IR> is being fit for that purpose (Sabelfeld and Dumay 2018). Thus, understanding some of the major developments that have shaped what <IR> represents today requires a journey that begins in post-apartheid South Africa.

2.1 South Africa: The Birthplace of Integrated Reporting

The origins of integrated reporting trace back much further than the IIRC's first Discussion Paper in 2011 (Rinaldi et al. 2018). In July 1993, under Nelson Mandela's presidency, Professor Mervyn King, a former Supreme Court judge, was asked by the Institute of Directors in South Africa (IoDSA) to chair the first official committee on corporate governance to increase corporate focus on transparency, equality, and information disclosure. In 1994, the commission, called the King Committee on Corporate Governance, released the first King Code of Corporate Governance Principles, commonly referred to as the King I Report (IoDSA 1994). Particularly noted for "its inclusive stakeholder (rather than merely shareholder) view of the corporation's ambit" (Gleeson-White 2014, p. 151), King I established a set of recommended standards for the conduct of board members in certain listed companies. The report strongly "encouraged companies to implement a Code of Ethics to demand 'the highest standards of behaviour'" (Eccles and Krzus 2014, p. 5). King I did not, however, call for environmental or social reporting, nor for linking matters relevant to those issues to financial performance.

It was not until the King II Report was released in 2002 that 'Integrated Sustainability Reporting' was introduced as a concept. A task force was established as

C. Bernardi, *Implementing Integrated Reporting*, SpringerBriefs in Accounting,
https://doi.org/10.1007/978-3-030-11193-9_2

a result of this report "to analyze a wide range of new and complex areas of non-financial reporting" (Gleeson-White 2014, p. 156). Inspired by the Johannesburg Earth Summit, the King II Report updated King I to include sections on sustainability, risk management, and the role of boards (Eccles and Krzus 2014, p. 6). King II urged organisations to broaden reporting beyond the financial dimension to include governance information as well as the environmental and social impacts of their activities. According to King II (IoDSA 2002, p. 96), sustainability sheds light on the non-financial aspects of business practice that have an impact on a company's "ability to survive and prosper within the communities within which it operates, and so ensure future value creation". King II explicitly embraced an inclusive stakeholder approach to corporate governance that required boards to consider the legitimate expectations of all its stakeholders when making decisions. The King II approach received international recognition as a leading corporate governance framework and, as a result, some of its principles were even incorporated into the Sarbanes-Oxley Act following the collapse of Enron and WorldCom (Gleeson-White 2014, p. 158). Following King II, the Johannesburg Stock Exchange Limited (JSE) required listed companies to include in their annual report a narrative statement explaining how they had complied with the King II principles or stating the reasons for non-compliance (IoDSA 2009, pp. 6–7).

By the time South Africa's New Companies Act (No. 71) passed in 2008, international trends in corporate governance had changed, which prompted a third report (Eccles and Krzus 2014). The King Report on Governance for South Africa King III (IoDSA 2009) was released in September 2009 and included the first set of established principles for integrated reporting. Integrated reports were advocated as "a holistic and integrated representation of the company's performance in terms of both its finances and its sustainability" (IoDSA 2009, p. 108). With King III, responsible corporate governance was taken one step further by explicitly recommending an integrated approach to reporting as a way to reflect the interconnections between business strategy, risk, performance, and sustainability. However, King III also departed from the rigid 'comply or explain' stance of the first two governance codes with a softer 'apply or explain' policy. As the King III Report itself noted, the transition would allow companies to use their own discretion but, at the same time, discourage 'tick-a-box' corporate governance reporting. Soon after, the JSE amended its listing requirements for the financial year starting on and after 1 March 2010 in accordance with King III's 'apply or explain' approach, making it compulsory for listed companies to comply with King III including the requirement of producing an integrated report or explain why not. In May 2010, the Integrated Reporting Committee of South Africa (IRCSA) was formed under the chairmanship of Professor Mervyn King with the purpose of providing specific direction and guidelines on how to prepare an integrated report and, in 2011, the world's first framework for preparing an integrated report was released by the IRCSA (IRCSA 2011).

In November 2016, the IoDSA, in tandem with the King Committee on Corporate Governance in South Africa, issued a fourth version of the Corporate Governance Code (IoDSA 2016) to replace its predecessor. Cognisant of the significant changes occurring within the corporate landscape, King IV revolves around the cornerstones of "ethical leadership, the organization in society, corporate citizenship, sustainable development, stakeholder inclusivity, integrated thinking and integrated reporting" (IoDSA 2016, p. 4). It builds on the philosophical foundations of King III but introduces several amendments to enhance its key concepts. In retrospect, it also embraces more of the elements that were to come with the impending <IR> movement. Abiding by King IV as the new Code for Corporate Governance has been stipulated on an 'apply and explain' basis. This new code requires companies to explain, in the form of a narrative account, which practices—as recommended by King IV (or other practices)—have been implemented and how they have contributed to achieving the good governance principles outlined by the Code. Companies are allowed to prepare an integrated report[1] in any form they choose, although the Code openly recommends the <IR> Framework as a good guide:

> *When drafting King IV, reliance was placed on the International <IR> Framework as issued by the International Integrated Reporting Council. The Integrated Reporting Committee of South Africa has endorsed the International <IR> Framework as good practice on how to prepare an integrated report and its further guidance on integrated reporting should be followed. (IoDSA* 2016*, p. 28)*

The key innovation of King IV lays in its underpinnings as a set of principles and outcomes rather than as a set of rules. The revised principles speak to the view that South African companies, for the most part, are already complying with King IV's principles, and that companies should aspire to the "mindful consideration and application of the recommended practices" (IoDSA 2016, p. 27). The universal applicability of King IV has been another appealing feature intended to contribute to its widespread adoption in South Africa. As the Report itself states, "good leadership, which is underpinned by the principles of good governance, is equally valuable in all types of organisations… [as] it talks of organisations and governing bodies, rather than simply companies and boards of directors" (IoDSA 2016, p. 6).

2.2 Integrated Reporting in the US

Another early exposition of integrated reporting is *One Report: Integrated Reporting for a Sustainable Strategy*, a book released in the US in 2010 by Eccles and Krzus (2010). *One Report* was written as a contribution to the "coordinated international response as occurred with the financial crisis to the environmental crisis" (Eccles and Krzus 2010, p. 9). Arguably, this variant of the integrated reporting concept, along with the recommendations in King III (IoDSA 2009), may have partly influenced

---

[1] According to King IV, an integrated report could either be "(i) a standalone report which connects the more detailed information in other reports, and addresses, at a high level and in a complete, concise way, the matters that could significantly affect the organisation's ability to create value; or (ii) a distinguishable, prominent and accessible part of another report which also includes the annual financial statements and other reports that must be issued in compliance with legal provisions" (IoDSA 2016, p. 48).

the ideas in the IIRC's Draft Framework released in 2011. However, as Tweedie (2014) points out, King III is primarily a corporate governance framework and One Report is a parallel development, neither of which are the same as the IIRC's concept of <IR>. Eccles and Krzus (2010, p. 10) outline that integrated reporting is much more than a mere combination of financial and non-financial information within a single annual document. They suggest that integrated reporting should combine Web 2.0 technologies with mainstream reports as, in this context, customised analysis by report users becomes key.

As of now, <IR> is still a foreign concept for most US firms. US companies already suffer heavily-regulated and burdensome reporting requirements. Hence, many seem hesitant to add <IR> to their disclosure overload (Adams 2018). Additionally, their current regulatory requirements do not significantly depart from the <IR> Framework in that companies must issue a 10-K report that provides an overview of the organisation's activities, risks, and financial performance (Adams 2018). Accordingly, one of Richard Howitt's main aims as the IIRC's CEO (2016–2019) has been to build support for <IR> in the US, where such a reporting practice appears to be unlikely to take hold and become mandatory, at least in the short term, given the existing regulatory burdens.

The low uptake of <IR> in the US particularly, and more generally internationally, is evidenced by the Corporate Register, which is the global online directory of corporate responsibility reports. In partnership with the IIRC, the Corporate Register provides a directory of reports that reference and align with the International <IR> Framework. More specifically, the corporateregister.com website classifies integrated reports registered with them at one of the following two levels:

(1) Level 1: The IIRC and/or the <IR> are referenced in the report.
(2) Level 2: The IIRC and/or the <IR> are referenced in the report, with at least two of the capitals as defined in the <IR> Framework being reported against.

According to their directory, disappointingly, only 30 US organisations published an integrated report during the period 2013–2017. Therefore, the evidence supports Adam's (2018) claim that the concept of <IR> is still foreign for most US firms.

2.3 The International Integrated Reporting Council

The IIRC emerged from the developments occurring in South Africa and the US and a need for the accounting profession to respond to the Global Financial Crisis (Gleeson-White 2014). In 2010, the establishment of the International Integrated Reporting Committee was announced in a joint press release by The Prince of Wales' Accounting for Sustainability Project (A4S) and the GRI. The Committee, ultimately convened as a Council in 2012 (i.e., the IIRC), was founded with the remit "to create a globally accepted framework for accounting for sustainability. A framework which brings together financial, environmental, social and governance information in a clear, concise, consistent and comparable format—put briefly, in an 'integrated' format" (A4S & GRI 2010, paragraph 3). Professor Mervyn King was appointed the Chairman to head the IIRC, with Paul Druckman, the former head of the Institute of Chartered Accountants of England and Wales, as its CEO. As such, the IIRC brought together a powerful cross-section of national and international representatives from the corporate, accounting, regulatory, securities, and standard-setting sectors.

The IIRC issued its first Discussion Paper on <IR> in September 2011 titled "Towards Integrated Reporting—Communicating Value in the 21st Century". The paper provided background information and the rationale behind <IR>, and announced the IIRC's intention to develop an <IR> Framework (IIRC 2011). Following the publication of a draft outline in June 2012, the first working draft of the <IR> Framework was released as a 'prototype' in November 2012. A consultation draft of the Framework was released in April 2013, which eventually led to a publicly-available feedback summary and, finally, the polished lt;IR> Framework was released in December 2013 (IIRC 2013a). Along the way, a disparate selection of resources was made available, including: a summary of the comments received about the initial Discussion Paper; background papers on materiality, the capitals, business models, value creation and connectivity; two IIRC Pilot Programme yearbooks; research (with Black Sun) on building the business case; and a database of emerging practice[2].

2.4 The International <IR> Framework

In the years since December 2013, the <IR> Framework has evolved in the context of increasing stakeholder scrutiny about the way companies create value and the potential risks associated with their activities. From the outset, the IIRC has tauted the <IR>Framework as the culmination of decades of development in financial, governance, management commentary, and sustainability reporting—tenets that both underpin and accelerate the evolution of corporate reporting (IIRC 2011).

The <IR> Framework is essentially a guide for organisations who wish to transition to <IR>. Further, the Framework sets out a philosophy whereby integrated reports represent "a concise communication about how an organization's strategy, governance, performance and prospects, in the context of its external environment, lead to the creation of value over the short, medium and long term" (IIRC 2013a, p. 1). According to the IIRC, an integrated report should be an organisation's "primary reporting vehicle" (IIRC 2011, p. 3) because it is concise, complete in all material respects, reliable, and unbiased in terms of the selection or presentation of information. Unlike standalone financial reports, the financial, social, and environmental information disclosed in an integrated report is interconnected (de Villiers et al. 2017). Hence, <IR> seeks to offer a broader picture of the modern organisation by shifting towards a document that contains holistic information on all the ways it creates value.

[2] http://examples.integratedreporting.org/home. Accessed October 13, 2019.

Far from being founded on a rigid rules-based approach, the <IR> Framework is principles-based, with the purpose of striking "an appropriate balance between flexibility and prescription that recognises the wide variation in individual circumstances of different organizations while enabling a sufficient degree of comparability across organizations to meet relevant information needs" (IIRC 2013a, pp. 4 and 12). However, the <IR> Framework contains little detailed information as to content. For example, it does not require the disclosure of any specific key performance indicators, measurement methods, or individual matters. Also, no specific structure is prescribed for preparing an integrated report as that should be determined by the organisation's unique value creation story. Similarly, the six capitals model is not intended to be unequivocal. Companies do not have to disclose information on all the capitals: which capitals they choose to report on is discretionary and should reflect the capitals most relevant to creating their value over the short-, medium-, and long-term.

What the <IR> Framework does do is identify the building blocks of an integrated report. Known as the 'Guiding Principles' and 'Content Elements', these ingredients form guidelines for what should be reported and how (IIRC 2013a, p. 5). The Guiding Principles, as defined in the 2013 <IR> Framework, are listed in Table 2.1, followed

Table 2.1 The Guiding Principles identified by the <IR> Framework

The Guiding Principles of <IR>
• **Strategic focus and future orientation** An integrated report should provide insight into (i) the organisation's strategy; (ii) how this strategy relates to the organisation's ability to create and sustain value over the short, medium and long term; and (iii) the strategy's use of and effects on the capitals the organization relies upon
• **Connectivity of information** An integrated report should provide a holistic picture of the interdependencies between the factors that affect the organisation's value creation process
• **Stakeholder relationships** An integrated report should provide insight into the nature and quality of the organisation's relationships with its key stakeholders and shed light on the organizations' responsiveness to the various stakeholders' information needs
• **Materiality** An integrated report should disclose information about those issues that have a substantial effect on the organisation's ability to create value over time
• **Conciseness** An integrated report should provide information in a succinct and clear way
• **Reliability and completeness** An integrated report should provide reliable, accurate and as complete as possible information
• **Consistency and comparability** The information in an integrated report should: (i) be presented in a consistent basis; (ii) be material to assessing the organization's ability to create and sustain value in the short, medium and long term; and (iii) enable comparison with other organizations

Source adapted from "The International <IR> Framework" (IIRC 2013a, p. 5)

Table 2.2 The Content Elements identified by the <IR> Framework

The Content Elements of <IR>
• **Organisational overview and external environment** Identification of the mission and vision of the organisation and the circumstances under which it operates
• **Governance** The organization's governance structure and how it supports the value creation process over the short, medium and long term
• **Business model** The organization's business model (i.e., the process by which value is created)
• **Risks and opportunities** Explanation of how the organisation is dealing with specific risks and opportunities that might affect the organisation's ability to create value over time
• **Strategy and resource allocation** The pursued organisational strategy and by which means it is going to be implemented
• **Performance** To what extent has the organization performed against its strategic objectives and what effect have the outcomes had on the various capitals
• **Outlook** The identification of potential challenges and future uncertainties that might prevent the organization from pursuing its strategy and their implications for its future performance
• **Basis of presentation** The criterion used by an organisation to determine what issues should be included in the integrated report and how such issues should be evaluated or quantified

Source adapted from "The International <IR> Framework" (IIRC 2013a, p. 5)

by the Content Elements in Table 2.2. Note that the Content Elements are not mutually exclusive—each is linked to the others.

The <IR> Framework revolves around three fundamental concepts: (i) the capitals that an organisation uses and affects; (ii) the organisation's business model and strategy; and (iii) the creation of value over the short-, medium-, and long-term. The IIRC takes a strong position on the matter of value creation: value is created over different time frames and for different stakeholders through different forms of capital (Fasan 2013, p. 53). In this regard, the <IR> Framework embodies the notion that the "value created by an organization over time manifests itself in increases, decreases or transformations of the capitals caused by the organization's business activities and outputs" (IIRC 2013a, p. 10).

Arguably, one of the most salient aspects of the <IR> Framework is its concept of "multiple capitals", which represent "stocks of value" (IIRC 2013a, p. 4). <IR> encourages companies to embrace a broader understanding of the value creation process by providing insights into one's own business strategy. Hence, its reporting should provide information on all the resources a firm takes as inputs and all the many capital outputs those inputs produce. The assumption behind the multi-capital approach is that, for many organisations, financial value alone is no longer sufficient for assessing success as, today, value creation increasingly relies on both tangible and intangible resources (IIRC 2013a). Therefore, by promoting accountability and stewardship, <IR> makes the interdependencies between a broad range of capitals visible. The <IR> Framework lists six different capitals it deems as playing a key role in value creation: financial, manufactured, social and relationship, intellectual, human, and natural. While not binding for disclosure, these capitals are intended to provide a more expansive basis for organisational management and reporting. Despite the emphasis placed on the multiple capitals concept, a great deal of concern has been raised by academics with respect to the fact that the IIRC does not provide specific guidance on how to measure any of these capitals. As Robertson and Samy (2015, p. 207) point out, this could result in subjective measurement eventually leaving room for disguising or even dismissing negative trade-offs.

The IIRC also recognises the business model as a central element of the <IR> Framework, defining it as "an organization's system of transforming inputs through its business activities into outputs and outcomes that aims to fulfil the organization's strategic purposes and create value over the short, medium and long term" (IIRC 2013a, p. 33). According to the IIRC, an accurate depiction of an organisational business model should provide investors and other interested stakeholders with insights into how the different capitals are used and how they contribute to value creation. A diagram from the <IR> Framework, shown as Fig. 2.1, provides a dynamic representation of the linkages between an organisation's business model and its ability to create value. In short, the business model takes input from the different types of capital and converts them into a range of outputs through business activities. Over time, this practice creates value for the organisation and outcomes beneficial to its

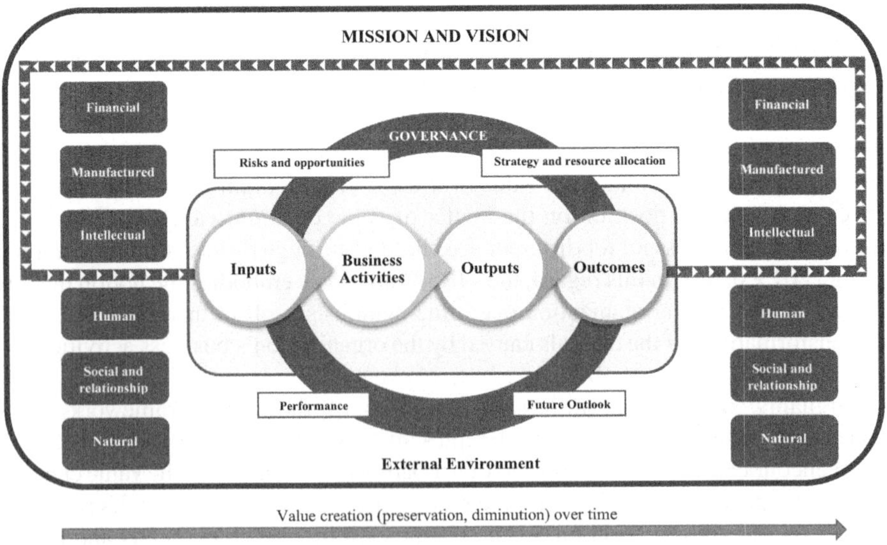

Fig. 2.1 The value creation process *Source* adapted from "The International <IR> Framework" (IIRC 2013a, p. 13)

stakeholders, the environment, and society as a whole. In this context, an integrated report recognises the importance of a broad range of capitals in developing a thorough understanding of an organisation's business model, which, in turn, leads to a concept the IIRC calls 'integrated thinking'.

Integrated thinking is integral to the <IR> Framework and can be reasonably regarded as all three of the foundation, the artefact, and the outcome of <IR> (Dumay et al. 2019). In fact, the IIRC's "long term vision is a world in which integrated thinking is embedded within mainstream business practice in the public and private sectors, facilitated by <IR> as the corporate reporting norm" (IIRC 2013a, p. 2). The IIRC itself claims that integrated thinking forms the basis of <IR>, and the two processes are "mutually reinforcing" (IIRC 2013b, p. 3). Accordingly, the <IR> Framework claims that significant changes and benefits do not come from the report itself, but rather from integrated thinking and the process of producing the report (IIRC 2011, 2013a). In this respect, Churet et al. (2014, p. 56) observe that "integrated reporting is only the tip of the iceberg. It is the visible part of what is happening below the surface—namely 'integrated thinking' and 'integrated decision-making'". Integrated thinking is a strategic and cultural approach to the management of an organisation. It requires companies to abandon their traditional silo mentality and take their various operational and functional units into consideration alongside the relevant capitals. Therefore, integrated thinking requires a thorough understanding of the process by which value is created, and that understanding should be translated into the company's business model. In this way, companies are better able to identify prospective risks and opportunities.

The IIRC's overarching goal to "explain to providers of financial capital how an organization creates value over time" (IIRC 2013a, p. 7, paragraph 1.7) suggests an investor-oriented perspective. Although providers of financial capital are identified as the primary target audience for <IR>, the IIRC (2013a, p. 7) claims that an integrated report, and other communications resulting from an integrated report, are of benefit to a wide spectrum of involved parties. Having passed through its so-called 'Breakthrough Phase' (2014–2017), however, the adoption of <IR> today is still arguably limited. Some companies have incorporated the <IR> Framework into their business practices, but regulated financial reports and separate, voluntary, environmental, social and governance reporting still remain the dominant reporting paradigm.

In keeping with the rollout of this strategy, the IIRC appointed Dominic Barton, Senior Partner and former Global Managing Partner of McKinsey & Company, to the post of Chairman in October 2018, and Professor Mervyn King's breakthrough charter has been superseded with a new 'Momentum Phase'. The goals of the 'Momentum Phase' "include advancing integrated thinking as part of corporate governance reform, facilitating alignment in the corporate reporting system and accelerating adoption in the United States and China" (IIRC 2018). It will be interesting to see how these efforts fair, especially in the US, given its hostility towards additional reporting burdens (Adams 2018). In support of this phase, the IIRC (2017) called for feedback from all stakeholders with knowledge of the <IR> Framework to gain insights into the enablers, incentives, and barriers that might impede its implementation. More than 400 submissions and contributions were received from a range of stakeholder groups, which have been packaged into a summary report titled "International <IR> Framework Implementation Feedback" (IIRC 2017) that provides first-hand feedback and evidence of how <IR> and integrated thinking are developing in practice.

Curiously, some feedback has been tagged for further investigation through a program of work, but no formal revisions were envisaged as being needed since "the feedback indicated that the Framework stands up well to the challenges of implementation" (IIRC 2017, p. 3). Just recently, during its November meeting in New York, the Council has confirmed "that wholesale changes should be avoided in favour of a simple modernization via minor corrections and clarifications" (IIRC News 2019). That there are no changes forthcoming is surprising considering the support (or lack thereof) for <IR> from the accounting profession. The feedback shows that core concepts such as understanding the six capitals and what is meant by integrated thinking are key issues, but these were not addressed in a revision even if just to clarify these concepts. It appears the IIRC is inextricably attached to the current <IR> Framework and is ignoring that some core concepts, like sunk costs, need revising. Arguably, the 'Momentum Phase' may also serve as evidence that the IIRC has still not achieved its goal of becoming the corporate reporting norm for the 'wide spectrum of involved parties' it seeks to benefit.

References

Adams, M. (2018). Emerging integrated reporting practices in the United States. In J. Guthrie, J. Dumay, F. Ricceri, & C. Nielsen (Eds.), *The routledge companion to intellectual capital: Frontiers of research, practice and knowledge* (pp. 365–379). London: Routledge.

Churet, C., RobecoSAM, A. G., & Eccles, R. G. (2014). Integrated reporting, quality of management, and financial performance. *Journal of Applied Corporate Finance, 26*(1), 56–64.

de Villiers, C., Hsiao, P.-C. K., & Warren, M. (2017). Developing a conceptual model of influences around integrated reporting, new insights and directions for future research. *Meditari Accountancy Research, 25*(4), 450–460. https://doi.org/10.1108/MEDAR-07-2017-0183.

Dumay, J., Bernardi, C., Guthrie, J., & La Torre, M. (2017). Barriers to implementing the International Integrated Reporting Framework: A contemporary academic perspective. *Meditari Accountancy Research, 25*(4), 461–480. https://doi.org/10.1108/MEDAR-05-2017-0150.

Dumay, J., La Torre, M., Bernardi, C., Guthrie, J. (2019). Integrated reporting and integrated thinking: Practical challenges. In S. Arvidsson (Ed.), *Challenges in managing sustainable business* (pp. 25–54). Cham: Palgrave Macmillan. https://doi.org/10.1007/978-3-319-93266-8_2.

Eccles, R., & Krzus, M. (2010). *One Report—Integrated reporting for a sustainable strategy*. Hoboken, New Jersey: Wiley.

Eccles, R. G., & Krzus, M. P. (2014). The integrated reporting movement: Meaning, momentum, motives, and materiality. Hoboken, New Jersey: Wiley.

Fasan, M. (2013). Annual reports, sustainability reports and integrated reports: Trends in corporate disclosure. In C. Busco, M. L. Frigo, A. Riccaboni, P. Quattrone, (Eds.), *Integrated reporting—Concepts and cases that redefine corporate accountability* (pp. 41–57). Switzerland: Springer International Publishing. https://doi.org/10.1007/978-3-319-02168-3.

Gleeson-White, J. (2014). *Six capitals: The revolution has to have–or can accountants save the planet?*. Sydney: Allen & Unwin.

International Integrated Reporting Committee (IIRC). (2011). Towards integrated reporting. Communicating value in the 21st century. International integrated reporting council, London. Available at: https://integratedreporting.org/wp-content/uploads/2011/09/IR-Discussion-Paper-2011_spreads.pdf (Accessed June 4, 2019).

International Integrated Reporting Council (IIRC). (2013a) The International framework, international integrated reporting council, London. Available at: http://www.integratedreporting.org/wp-content/uploads/2015/03/13-12-08-THE-INTERNATIONAL-IR-FRAMEWORK-2-1.pdf. (Accessed July 4, 2019).

International Integrated Reporting Council (IIRC) (2013b). Connectivity: Background paper for <IR>. Available at: https://integratedreporting.org/wp-content/uploads/2013/07/IR-Background-Paper-Connectivity.pdf (Accessed August 22, 2019).

International Integrated Reporting Council (IIRC) (2017). International <IR> framework implementation feedback: Invitation to comment. International integrated reporting council, London. Available at: https://integratedreporting.org/invitation-to-comment/(Accessed August 18, 2019).

International Integrated Reporting Council (IIRC) (2018). Dominic Barton appointed as chair of international integrated reporting council, as new strategic phase is launched. Available at: https://integratedreporting.org/news/dominic-barton-appointed-as-chair-of-international-integrated-reporting-council-as-new-strategic-phase-is-launched/ (Accessed September 16, 2018).

IIRC Newsletter. (2019). International <IR> framework to be revised in 2020. Available at: https://mailchi.mp/theiirc/iirc-newsletter-690533?e=1c5c47be87#Revised. 3 December 2019 (Accessed December 4, 2019).

Institute of Directors in Southern Africa (IoDSA). (1994). The King Report on Corporate Governance (King I), Johannesburg.

Institute of Directors in Southern Africa (IoDSA). (2002). The King Report on Corporate Governance for South Africa (King II), Johannesburg.

Institute of Directors in Southern Africa (IoDSA). (2009). Report on Corporate Governance for South Africa (King III), Johannesburg. Available at: https://www.iodsa.co.za/page/KingIII (Accessed June 27, 2019).

Institute of Directors in Southern Africa (IoDSA). (2016). Report on Corporate Governance for South Africa (King IV), Johannesburg. https://www.adams.africa/wp-content/uploads/2016/11/King-IV-Report.pdf (Accessed August 26, 2019).

Integrated Reporting Committee of South Africa (IRCSA). (2011). Framework for integrated reporting and the integrated report. Available at: http://integratedreportingsa.org/ircsa/wp-content/uploads/2017/05/IRC-of-SA-Integrated-Reporting-Guide-Jan-11.pdf (Accessed September 24, 2019).

Prince's Accounting for Sustainability Project (A4S) and Global Reporting Initiative (GRI). (2010). Formation of the International Integrated Reporting Committee (IIRC). Available at: https://integratedreporting.org/wp-content/uploads/2011/03/Press-Release1.pdf (Accessed October 3, 2019).

Rinaldi, L., Unerman, J., & de Villiers, C. (2018). Evaluating the integrated reporting journey: Insights, gaps and agendas for future research. *Accounting, Auditing & Accountability Journal, 31*(5), 1294–1318. https://doi.org/10.1108/AAAJ-04-2018-3446.

Robertson, F. A., & Samy, M. (2015). Factors affecting the diffusion of integrated reporting-A UK FTSE 100 perspective. *Sustainability Accounting, Management and Policy Journal, 6*(2), 190–223. https://doi.org/10.1108/SAMPJ-07-2014-0044.

Sabelfeld, S., Dumay, J. (2018). *Adoption of integrated reporting: Lost in local translation?* Paper presented at the Financial Reporting Workshop, University of Bologna, 14–15 June 2018.

Tweedie, D. (2014). Integrated reporting: Symptom or cure of new capitalism's ills?. In *Proceedings of the Critical Perspectives on Accounting Conference, Toronto*, 7–9 July 2014.

Chapter 3
The Stages of <IR> Research

Abstract Like its predecessor, intellectual capital, <IR> was initially conceived by practitioners with academics following closely behind in either support or opposition. This chapter outlines the two sides of the debate and, through this analysis, also explores the stages of <IR> research as well as the relationship between practitioners and academics. Commonly, first-stage research in a field is simply explorations of concepts and ideas, while second-stage research addresses our understanding of their ostensive impacts. Third-stage of research critically examines how to implement the ideas refined in the first- and second-stages. In this sense, the path from first to third-stage research can be likened to the bridge that must be crossed between practitioners and academics for an idea to truly succeed. This is the journey to be explored in this chapter.

3.1 Practitioners, Academics and <IR>

Nothing can exemplify the opposing quarter's sentiments towards <IR> better than Milne and Gray's (2013, p. 20) declaration:

> *The IIRC's discussion paper, Towards Integrated Reporting is a masterpiece of obfuscation and avoidance of any recognition of the prior 40 years of research and experimentation. Despite its claims for sustainable development and sustainability, it is exclusively investor focused and it has virtually nothing—and certainly nothing substantive—to say about either accountability or sustainability. Should IR take over from GRI and the TBL [Triple Bottom Line] as the focus of choice, then we will be heading even further away from any plausible possibility that sustainability might be seriously embraced by any element of business and politics.*

Whether or not you agree with Milne and Gray, it is clear that <IR> is not a trivial movement and, for this very reason, its existence and impact merit investigation. However, there are some significant challenges researchers and practitioners need to overcome because, like the intellectual capital (IC) movement, <IR> is a practitioner-driven concept. In the early days of IC, prominent names like Karl-Erik Sveiby (1989), Thomas Stewart (1991), and Leif Edvinsson (1997) were some of the leading thinkers and practitioners. These professionals and their contemporaries were advocating a revolution in the way companies were managed. They wanted

C. Bernardi, *Implementing Integrated Reporting*, SpringerBriefs in Accounting,
https://doi.org/10.1007/978-3-030-11193-9_3

worth to be recognised as including the value of knowledge and intangible assets, in addition to money. These intangible assets are now commonly referred to as intellectual capital and broken down into a series of sub capitals depending on the framework or definition at hand—for example, the six capitals of <IR> or human, relational, and structural capital as the three most common.

Similarly, <IR> was founded by accountants who were concerned with the impacts of the Global Financial Crisis and how companies needed to better communicate their value creation stories (Gleeson-White 2014). Interestingly, that the initiative is led by accountants is also the basis of one of the prime concerns over <IR>, i.e., that it has been 'captured' by the accounting profession and has forgotten about its original altruistic management principles—that it places financial sustainability before social and environmental sustainability (Flower 2015). Likewise, Brown and Dillard (2014 p. 1147), explicitly state that <IR>"may code well with mainstream accounting and existing governance structures that privilege finance capital" but "is likely to take us ever further away from social and environmental reporting that might promote corporate accountability, stakeholder empowerment, democratic governance and sustainability." Nevertheless, despite these concerns, it appears that there are also many academics that support the IIRC and <IR>. For example, Adams (2015, p. 23) argues for "integrated reporting and its potential to change the thinking of corporate actors leading to the further integration of sustainability actions and impacts into corporate strategic planning and decision making".

Given that both IC and <IR> research began in response to a practitioner idea, a lesson to be learned from IC research is that academics need to quickly move on from advocating good ideas to critically evaluating <IR>'s merits. Only through critical research can ideas like <IR> be improved, and it is the job of academics to carry out unbiased research to achieve that evaluation. To make a significant research contribution to <IR>, academics need to engage more with practice. Accounting researchers have long been accused of conducting research that contributes little to practice, if anything at all. They tend not to investigate specific processes or specific organisations, and they do not engage to a great extent with practitioners as collaborators. This has been a major challenge for accounting in general (Evans et al. 2011), and research into <IR> appears to be no different. As Tucker and Lowe (2014) contend, at times, "practitioners are from Mars and academics are from Venus". To counter the divide between researchers and practitioners, more performative (Mouritsen 2006) and interventionist research is needed (Jönsson and Lukka 2005; Dumay 2010). Academics must start getting their hands dirty if they are to help organisations understand whether the concepts of <IR>, such as integrated thinking, can live up to the IIRC's ideology.

If academics unquestioningly accept <IR> as the future corporate reporting norm, they are merely joining the chorus of practitioners who advocate <IR> as "the next step in the evolution of corporate reporting" (IIRC 2013). If academics and practitioners accept the IIRC's rhetorical arguments on face value and do not question <IR> in practice, we may find ourselves in a vicious circle of reporting that does not create value, but rather destroys it. Moreover, universities, think tanks, and organisations are at risk of wasting time, effort, and money on research and reporting that might have no, or very little, impact. Fortunately, more critical research is coming to the fore, which suggests that academics are not accepting the IIRC's ideology too easily, but rather engaging critically with <IR>'s concepts as a guide to genuinely evaluate its effectiveness.

3.2 The "<IR> Agenda"

The next issue to consider is the "<IR > agenda" as espoused by the IIRC, which some critics like Flower (2015) allege is more of "a hidden agenda".[1] Although arguments claiming the existence of a hidden agenda have a point, the IIRC's agenda may not be quite as hidden as one might think. In fact, it is plain for all to see if one only looks. The IIRC may not act entirely as a honest broker, but there is evidence in favour of its arguments that do not come in the form of a simple list of <IR>'s advantages and disadvantages. A key issue here is that, since its inception, the IIRC has used its substantial financial resources to promote research in favour of <IR>. For example, since publishing its Discussion Paper (IIRC 2011) and the <IR> Framework (IIRC 2013), the IIRC has published self-funded research in the guise of two reports outlining the benefits of <IR> (Black Sun 2012, 2014). Within these reports, the IIRC comments: "We are grateful to Black Sun for initiating and conducting the research to help us track these changes which provide clear evidence of the business benefits of Integrated Reporting" (Black Sun 2012, p. 1) and "The business case for Integrated Reporting is very clear from our latest research, in partnership with communications consultancy Black Sun 'Realizing the benefits: The impact of Integrated Reporting', which builds on our initial research in 2012" (Black Sun 2014, p. 1).

This research is intended to argue for <IR>'s benefits. What is interesting, however, is that it was produced by a public relations company as opposed to a bonafide and independent scholar or an academic consultancy. Black Sun's main competency, presumably, is promotion, and the reports do look more like marketing documents. Not a single word detracts from <IR>'s benefits and the arguments are couched in evocative language with coloured graphics designed to make <IR> appealing. As outlined by Black Sun (2014, p. 27) "Black Sun is one of Europe's leading strategic corporate communications consultancies. Founded in 1991, it brings together corporate reporting, sustainability and digital communications to create powerful integrated solutions for clients". Additionally, given that Black Sun is a public relations company, it quite reasonably offers an extensive disclaimer on the back page of both reports (Black Sun 2012, p. 30; Black Sun 2014, p. 30):

> *All information in this report is provided 'as is' and Black Sun Plc provides no warranties or representations as to the completeness, accuracy or suitability for any purpose of the content of this report or any other warranty of any kind, express or implied, including but not limited to, warranties of satisfactory quality, non-infringement, or compatibility. Therefore, Black*

[1] Abeit, Flower (2015, p. 16) does note that "Since, by definition, their agenda is hidden, it is not possible to prove my claim conclusively."

Sun Plc distances itself from its own IR research findings should any organisation believe and act upon the espoused benefits outlined in these reports, and suffer a loss.

A suspicious person might ask why the IIRC produced these reports. However, the answer is found in the methodology sections of both reports, where the IIRC states: "As all the participants are already working towards <IR>, their responses are likely to be more positive about it as an approach than those of a random selection of organizations would be" (Black Sun 2012, p. 26; Black Sun 2014, p. 26). If such reports were submitted to an academic journal as a paper, reviewers would highly likely reject the findings as biased unless that issue was handled very carefully in the author(s)' interpretation. In the case of these two reports, it is not clear whether bias was indeed handled with care.

Taking the idea behind this methodology to the extreme, the approach used in these reports can be likened to the idea of going to a church and asking the congregation if they believe in God. Much of the results for the companies analysed may be genuine, but the sample is not representative of the overall population, and an unrepresentative sample usually leads to misleading conclusions that have little use for the field or firms. More importantly, this contrasts with the situation faced by academics, who must wait until their work passes review through the editorial gates of rigour before finding its way into the public domain. Even then, the lack of open access to academic journals means opportunities for the public to access reliable, peer-reviewed <IR> research is somewhat limited. Whether academics can devise methods of promulgating their research that match the reach of the IIRC is a point worthy of debate. Putting forward research that has not been conducted by independent researchers based on a biased sample, and without taking that bias into consideration when drawing conclusions, is not the work of an honest broker. Arguably, the IIRC has used its money and power to publish self-serving research to further its agenda and reach potential stakeholders as and when desired.

In a related vein, a considerable number of practitioners and academics have supported the research to promote the IIRC's agenda, such as the original calls for research proposals by the ACCA (Association of Chartered Certified Accountants) and the IAAER (International Association for Accounting Education and Research). Further, the IIRC seems to seek research to support the further development of <IR>, rather than objective critiques. In this context, an academic applying for research funds would need to at least give the impression of agreeing in principle with <IR> . Evidence for this argument is supplied by the ACCA itself, which only looked for research proposals "as part of its ongoing funding for international accounting research, and its support for the work of both IAAER and IIRC" (2014, p. 2). However, from the research community there have been more than a few papers that have been relatively critical of <IR> and its accomplishments (see, for example, Higgins et al. 2014; van Bommel 2014; Flower 2015; Thomson 2015; Rowbottom and Locke 2016; Dumay and Dai 2017), while some academics remain ardent supporters (e.g., Adams 2015, 2017). Arguably, both academia and the accounting profession would benefit more from a rigorous investigation of <IR>'s positive and negative attributes. Without an open evaluation, no new critical insights are possible; no new contributions to further <IR>'s potential can be offered at the risk of <IR> remaining unchanged and inevitably stagnate. As La Torre et al. (2019, p. 17) outline, there still is "insufficient evidence of its benefits, a controversial shift in its underpinning ideology, and a lack of traditional sources of regulatory power and legitimation".

Another aspect of how the IIRC has pursued its agenda, is how it has interacted with existing organisations in the crowded field of environmental and social reporting. For example, although the GRI predates the IIRC by around 13 years, Eccles and Krzus (2014) argue that the GRI has gradually been assimilating <IR> into its mandate since the IIRC was formed. A Memorandum of Understanding (MoU), signed by GRI Chief Executive Ernst Ligteringen and IIRC Chief Executive Officer Paul Druckman in March 2013 supports this claim as it testifies to the shared interest of both organisations in enhancing the evolution of corporate reporting. That said, Humphrey et al. (2017, p. 49) highlight that a more accurate analysis of the commitments and arrangements between the parties reveals that the MoU was drafted with care to ensure neither of the participating bodies would threaten the other's future plans for development:

> *The IIRC commits to (...) develop and maintain the International <IR> Framework with the intent that it will be (to the extent relevant, applicable and practicable) compatible with and supportive of, yet avoiding duplication (where reasonably possible) of, GRI's guidelines and standards, both current and (to the extent reasonable and practicable) under development.*
>
> *GRI commits to (...) develop and maintain its guidelines and standards with the intent that these will be (to the extent relevant, applicable and practicable) compatible with and supportive of the International <IR> Framework and related guidance, both current and (to the extent reasonable and practicable) under development.*

Notably, the IIRC has entered into numerous alliances with competing reporting and standard-setting bodies under a MoU, such as the International Federation of Accountants (IFAC), the International Accounting Standards Board (IASB), the Carbon Disclosure Project (CDP), the Climate Disclosure Standards Board (CDSB), the World Intellectual Capital Initiative (WICI), and the Sustainability Accounting Standards Board (SASB) (Humphrey et al. 2017). Similar to the MoU signed with the GRI, these arrangements reflect a common interest between the parties but, at the same time, their wording provides assurances that <IR> will not interfere with existing reporting spaces. Therefore, it is questionable whether the IIRC and the involved parties are genuinely seeking to co-contribute to a global reporting framework or whether they are trying not to step on each other's toes while defending their existing positions.

Further, the IIRC does not present <IR> as the 'next generation' of sustainability reporting. <IR> is promoted as "a more cohesive and efficient approach to corporate reporting that draws on different reporting strands" (IIRC 2013, p. 2). Certainly, there are similarities between the IIRC and the GRI. For example, the GRI states that "although the objectives of sustainability reporting and integrated reporting may be different, sustainability reporting is an intrinsic element of integrated reporting" (GRI 2013 p. 85). Also, the target audiences for <IR> and sustainability reporting are touted to be substantially different. Sustainability reporting aims to provide social, environmental, and economic information to the vast array of stakeholders associated with a company, while the primary aim of <IR> is to explain how an organisation creates value over time to providers of financial capital (IIRC 2013). Overall, it is clear that the IIRC has adopted a sophisticated political strategy to advance its conception of <IR> as the future corporate norm of financial reporting by avoiding 'turf wars' with other parties operating in the same or similar integrated reporting domains. Free from these distractions, the IIRC has been able to concentrate on its own agenda (Humphrey et al. 2017).

3.3 Support and Critique

The accounting profession, especially the ACCA, is firmly committed to the benefits of <IR> as outlined by the IIRC. As the ACCA website[2] discloses:

> *The International Reporting Council (IIRC) has its headquarters at ACCA and issued a draft framework for the practice of financial reporting in April 2013, which has formed the basis for ACCA to develop more IR content within its syllabuses, particularly at the Professional level. This will take place with effect from December 2014.*
>
> To lead this initiative, ACCA is planning to incorporate learning outcomes relating to the suggested outcomes of an integrated report.

This statement suggests that the ACCA is implementing <IR> training without any solid evidence of its benefits. From an educational perspective, this is worrying—especially if the IIRC is creating a cohort of <IR> disciples through the ACCA based on suggested outcomes as opposed to outcomes solidly grounded in critical academic research. While it cannot be denied that there is a place for the normative arguments presented by the IIRC, it is unethical to indoctrinate accounting practitioners into believing that <IR> will attain certain goals without any rigorous evidence to support this case. Depicting the small and, as yet, immature reality of <IR> as capable of single-handedly and radically changing how we manage organisations is a proposition based on the butterfly effect. However, based on evidence in research that critiques the potential of <IR> (Flower 2015; Thomson 2015; Rowbottom and Locke 2016; Dumay and Dai 2017; La Torre et al. 2019), depending on the butterfly effect is a long bow to draw.

It is also worth pointing out that teaching <IR> to prospective accounting professionals is a good strategy for proliferating the IIRC's agenda. Instilling the new generation with <IR> truths in the very foundations of a curriculum has a great deal of merit in this respect. As Dumay and Adams (2014) argue, one of the reasons why IC did not penetrate and, consequently, proliferate into management practice was because of preaching by academics. A grand theory linking IC to value creation was never proven, leaving only words in its support (Dumay 2012). The same is true with a grand theory that links <IR> to value creation. With lessons well-learned, 'heretic' academics should concentrate on developing research with the accounting

[2]https://www.accaglobal.com/hk/en/student/sa/features/acca-embeds-integrated-reporting.html. Accessed September 12, 2019.

profession not despite them (Bourdieu 1977), because it is only through rigorous empirical research that the IIRC's rhetoric can be replaced with knowledge worth accepting and teaching.

3.4 Future Research Agenda

This chapter, and its pessimistic critique, would be lacking an important aspect without proposing a way forward for <IR> research. Academic research into <IR> is increasing, and while this is not necessarily a negative thing, at the moment, there does seem to be more academics interested in <IR> than organisations. However, more research that engages critically with <IR>'s rhetoric and practice is needed. To frame the following discussion around a list of priorities for future <IR> research, it is useful to draw parallels with the closely related field of IC research which has developed through four distinct research stages (Dumay and Garanina 2013).

3.4.1 Moving Beyond First-Stage Research

Petty and Guthrie (2000, pp. 155–156) maintain that:

> *First-stage efforts have typically focused on consciousness raising activities that strive to communicate the importance of recognising and understanding the potential for (...) creating and managing a sustainable competitive advantage. The aim of stage one [is] to render the invisible visible by creating a discourse that all could engage in.*

This argument is reflected in early <IR> research, which was primarily concerned with processes for establishing and promoting <IR>'s guidelines (see, for example, Cheng et al. 2014). With the creation of the IIRC and its numerous sponsored publications (e.g. Black Sun 2012, 2014) and early-stage normative research, it is reasonable to say the first-stage of <IR> research has come of age. Further, subsequent research in this direction has offered few new insights, and so it is now time to test the IIRC's rhetoric.

Unfortunately, <IR> research has not yet fully progressed to its second-stage, where <IR> is established as a legitimate undertaking. Robust evidence is still being gathered in support of its further development. That said, it would be unfair to criticise research for not yet proving the merits of <IR>, as it is still in its early days. The first official <IR> guideline was only released in December 2013, and there are still not enough examples of companies who have or are implementing <IR> in practice. However, the few second-stage studies firmly establish that implementing <IR> has its own set of barriers to overcome (Dumay et al. 2017) and that the impact and benefits of <IR> are fragmented and inconclusive. Should more companies adopt <IR> over time, this will open up a fuller corpus of opportunities for research to progress beyond the first-stage process and engagement. The South African site might provide an opportunity here, given its experimentation with <IR>. Thus, there is potential for further research that focuses on understanding the history, emergence, and future of the <IR> project.

3.4.2 Third-Stage <IR> Research: Bridging the Gap Between Practice and Academia

According to Guthrie et al. (2012, p. 69), third-stage research is "based on a critical and performative analysis of IC practices in action". However, this may be a linear view. Second- and third-stage research can co-exist. While second-stage studies address our understanding of the ostensive impacts of <IR>, third-stage research can concurrently focus on performative <IR> because acknowledging that the antecedents of today's <IR> movement lie in practice provides an important reminder to academics to keep their work relevant to the profession. In fact, there is already an emerging body of literature that could be considered as the beginnings of third-stage research. For example, there is a growing academic debate on the challenges associated with implementing <IR> (e.g., Dumay et al. 2017; McNally et al. 2017). Focussed on the preparers of integrated reports, Dumay et al. (2017) highlight the barriers and difficulties associated with implementing <IR>. McNally et al. (2017, p. 481) find that implementing <IR> is problematic because it is not perceived as a natural part of a business process since it "is imposed on existing internal processes and reporting protocols which preclude a broad understanding of the purpose of integrated reporting and limit the development of management control systems". Thus, to many companies, implementing <IR> either means it supersedes another reporting process or becomes an additional reporting burden.

Within the context of public service organisations, Guthrie et al. (2017) investigate the internal mechanisms of change that can lead organisations to adopt <IR> and what impact, if any, it has on integrated thinking. Their findings suggest that <IR> "can be considered more as an incremental phase in sustainability reporting rather than a ground-breaking transformation of the existing financial and sustainability reporting approaches already mature in the organisations" (p. 568). <IR> for small and medium-sized enterprises (SMEs) has received little attention so far. One exception is research by Del Baldo (2017), who provides insights into the most critical aspects SMEs encounter when operationalising <IR>. Her findings suggest that the main challenges SMEs face include: identifying the relationship between <IR> and sustainability reporting; the process of adapting <IR> concepts to suit their own needs; and the lack of a proper understanding of <IR>'s potential benefits.

Rinaldi et al. (2018) analyse the overall journey of <IR> as envisaged by the IIRC. Their analysis reveals that most of the focus has been on final production, not the journey. Such studies would open up the opportunity for fourth-stage research, which centres on how <IR> impacts entire ecosystems, i.e., networks of stakeholders, countries, and regions. Here, too, there is an emerging research agenda with studies exploring how and why <IR> is spreading across emerging markets, such as Sri Lanka (Gunarathne and Senaratne 2017), Taiwan (Hsiao and Kelly 2018), Colombia (Macias and Farfan-Lievano 2017), and more established countries, such as Japan (Sabelfeld and Dumay 2018). However, more research is needed to understand why particular countries adopt and adapt <IR> to suit local needs.

Researchers and practitioners alike often bemoan the dissociation between what researchers investigate and what businesses want to know (Evans et al. 2011). Being a part of a research movement at its genesis provides a perfect opportunity to bridge this gap. For instance, at a regulatory level, widespread acceptance and possible future mandatory <IR> requirements are only likely to occur with solid and rigorous evidence of <IR>'s advantages to stakeholders. Should <IR> prove beneficial for companies and economies, then governments and regulators will have both evidence and justification for regulating or recommending <IR> as a corporate reporting guideline. However, given that similar calls on behalf of IC over the last two decades have not resulted in mandates, recommendation is more likely than regulation. Thus, harmonising <IR> with financial reporting still seems a distant dream.

Recent developments in Europe, such as the EU Directive (Directive 2014/95/EU), may be a last saviour for mandating <IR> on the continent (Dumay et al. 2017). No Member State has yet recommended <IR> as a framework for complying with the Directive, despite the appointment of Richard Howitt as the IIRC's CEO in 2016. Howitt was not only previously a Member of the European Parliament but also the architect of the EU Directive (Monciardini et al. 2016). To date, the GRI appears to be the favourite among competing frameworks given it is already well-established and has also issued specific guidelines on how to comply with the 2014 EU Directive (GRI and Global Sustainability Standards Board 2017).

Ongoing attempts to globalise an integrated reporting standard also raises interesting questions about the ability to harmonise <IR> with financial accounting. When practice leads the way and policy follows suit, numerous issues need to be agreed upon. For example, experimentation with <IR> practices is on the increase in Europe, Japan, and Australia, but few comparative studies examine the diversity of <IR> practice. The motivations behind an organisation's decision to report non-financial material in conjunction with their existing obligations is also under-explored. These experimentations with the <IR> project should produce more research over time that reveals the influence of <IR> on the practice of accounting, how <IR> is adopted, and how financial and non-financial information is used both internally and externally. Consider this a call in support of Beck et al. (2017) position for research into these aspects of <IR>, particularly the corporate reporting journey that companies take towards <IR> and beyond.

The policies embodied within the <IR> guidelines also raise further questions. Should the guidelines be prescriptive or normative? Should more elements within each of the capitals be specified? Which metrics could be used to communicate those elements? The prescriptive nature of <IR> is an important issue because it leans towards the need for greater education on <IR> and its various capitals, especially when it comes to implementing a strategy, creating value, and preserving those capitals. If users are <IR> illiterate, then <IR> has no value. Hence, external audiences need to be better educated with a broader understanding of the issues associated with <IR> and how to interpret the fundamental concepts that underpin it.

Additionally, given the differences in organisational types and activities, considerable fluidity and flexibility will have to be built into any guidelines and standards. The experience of the GRI indicates that industry-based guidelines could be a way to proceed. For example, the GRI guidelines have considerable individual metrics that are contextually specific because it is difficult for one overarching guideline to cover a universal set of organisations and business activities. Yet, despite some success in this customised approach, evidence from research on the GRI shows that industry take-up has still been slow and haphazard (see Dumay et al. 2010). Thus, the IIRC should pay attention to the lessons learned from similar frameworks, such as the GRI and IC reporting, to avoid the same problems and issues.

References

ACCA (Association of Chartered Certified Accountants) and IAAER (International Association for Accounting Education and Research). (2014). *Call for research proposals: Integrated reporting*. Available at: file:///D:/BOOK%20Springer_October%202019/October%202019/Handover/ACCA_IIRC_IAAER_CFP.pdf. Accessed October 2, 2019.

Adams, C. A. (2015). The International Integrated Reporting Council: A call to action. *Critical Perspectives on Accounting, 27,* 23–28. https://doi.org/10.1016/j.cpa.2014.07.001.

Adams, C. A. (2017). *Understanding integrated reporting: The concise guide to integrated thinking and the future of corporate reporting*. New York: Routledge.

Beck, C., Dumay, J., & Frost, G. (2017). In pursuit of a 'single source of truth': From threatened legitimacy to integrated reporting. *Journal of Business Ethics, 141*(1), 191–205. https://doi.org/10.1007/s10551-014-2423-1.

Black Sun (2012). *Understanding transformation: Building the business case for integrated reporting*. International Integrated Reporting Council, London. Available at: https://integratedreporting.org/wp-content/uploads/2012/11/BUILDING-THE-BUSINESS-CASE-FOR-INTEGRATED-REPORTING.pdf. Accessed September 18, 2019.

Black Sun (2014). *Realizing the benefits: The impact of integrated reporting*. International Integrated Reporting Council, London. Available at: https://integratedreporting.org/wp-content/uploads/2014/09/IIRC.Black_.Sun_.Research.IR_.Impact.Single.pages.18.9.14.pdf. Accessed September 27, 2019.

Bourdieu, P. (1977). *Outline of a theory of practice*. Cambridge: Cambridge University Press.

Brown, J., & Dillard, J. (2014). Integrated reporting: On the need for broadening out and opening up. *Accounting, Auditing and Accountability Journal, 27*(7), 1120–1156. https://doi.org/10.1108/AAAJ-04-2013-1313.

Cheng, M., Green, W., Conradie, P., Konishi, N., & Romi, A. (2014). The international integrated reporting framework: Key issues and future research opportunities. *Journal of International Financial Management and Accounting, 25*(1), 90–119.

Del Baldo, M. (2017). The implementation of integrating reporting <IR> in SMEs. *Meditari Accountancy Research, 25*(4), 505–532. https://doi.org/10.1108/MEDAR-11-2016-0094.

Dumay, J. (2010). A critical reflective discourse of an interventionist research project. *Qualitative Research in Accounting and Management, 7*(1), 46–70. https://doi.org/10.1108/11766091011034271.

Dumay, J. (2012). Grand theories as barriers to using IC concepts. *Journal of Intellectual Capital, 13*(1), 4–15. https://doi.org/10.1108/14691931211196187.

Dumay, J., & Adams, M. (2014). The learning journey of IC missionaries: Intuition, control and value creation. *The Electronic Journal of Knowledge Management, 12*(2), 135–143.

Dumay, J., & Dai, T. (2017). Integrated thinking as a cultural control? *Meditari Accountancy Research, 25*(4), 574–604. https://doi.org/10.1108/MEDAR-07-2016-0067.

Dumay, J., & Garanina, T. (2013). Intellectual capital research: A critical examination of the third stage. *Journal of Intellectual Capital, 14*(1), 10–25. https://doi.org/10.1108/14691931311288995.

Dumay, J., Guthrie, J., & Farneti, F. (2010). GRI sustainability reporting guidelines for public and third sector organisations: A critical review. *Public Management Review, 12*(4), 531–548. https://doi.org/10.1080/14719037.2010.496266.

Dumay, J., Bernardi, C., Guthrie, J., & La Torre, M. (2017). Barriers to implementing the international integrated reporting framework: A contemporary academic perspective. *Meditari Accountancy Research, 25*(4), 461–480. https://doi.org/10.1108/MEDAR-05-2017-0150.

Eccles, R. & Krzus, M. (2014). The integrated reporting movement. meaning, momentum, motives, and materiality. Hoboken, New Jersey: Wiley & Sons, Inc.

Edvinsson, L. (1997). Developing intellectual capital at Skandia. *Long Range Planning, 30,* 366–373.

European Union. (2014). Directive 2014/95/EU of the European Parliament and of the Council. Available at: https://eur-lex.europa.eu/legal-content/EN/TXT/?uri=CELEX%3A32014L0095.

Evans, E., Burritt, R. & Guthrie, J. (2011). *Bridging the gap between academic accounting research and professional practice*. Sydney and Adelaide: Institute of Charted Accountants in Australia, Sydney and Centre for Accounting, Governance and Sustainability, University of South Australia.

Flower, J. (2015). The international integrated reporting council: A story of failure. *Critical Perspectives on Accounting, 27,* 1–17. https://doi.org/10.1016/j.cpa.2014.07.002.

Gleeson-White, J. (2014). *Six capitals: The revolution capitalism has to have—or can accountants save the planet?*. Sydney: Allen and Unwin.

Global Reporting Initiative (GRI). (2013). *G4: Sustainability reporting guidelines*. Reporting principles and standard disclosures. Available at: https://www2.globalreporting.org/resourcelibrary/GRIG4-Part1-Reporting-Principles-and-Standard-Disclosures.pdf. Accessed October 13, 2019.

GRI & Global Sustainability Standards Board. (2017). Linking the GRI Standards and the European Directive on non-financial and diversity disclosure. Amsterdam. Available at: https://www.globalreporting.org/standards/resource-download-center/linking-gri-standards-and-european-directive-on-non-financial-and-diversity-disclosure/. Accessed October 4, 2019.

Gunarathne, N., & Senaratne, S. (2017). Diffusion of integrated reporting in an emerging South Asian (SAARC) nation. *Managerial Auditing Journal, 32*(4/5), 524–548. https://doi.org/10.1108/MAJ-01-2016-1309.

Guthrie, J., Ricceri, F., & Dumay, J. (2012). Reflections and projections: A decade of intellectual capital accounting research. *The British Accounting Review, 44*(2), 68–82. https://doi.org/10.1016/j.bar.2012.03.004.

Guthrie, J., Manes-Rossi, F., & Orelli, R. L. (2017). Integrated reporting and integrated thinking in Italian public sector organisations. *Meditari Accountancy Research, 25*(4), 553–573. https://doi.org/10.1108/MEDAR-06-2017-0155.

Higgins, C., Stubbs, W., & Love, T. (2014). Walking the talk(s): Organisational narratives of integrated reporting. *Accounting, Auditing and Accountability Journal, 27*(7), 1090–1119. https://doi.org/10.1108/AAAJ-04-2013-1303.

Hsiao, P.-C. K., & Kelly, M. (2018). Investment considerations and impressions of integrated reporting: Evidence from Taiwan. *Sustainability Accounting, Management and Policy Journal, 9*(1), 2–28. https://doi.org/10.1108/SAMPJ-10-2016-0072.

Humphrey, C., O'Dwyer, B., & Unerman, J. (2017). Re-theorizing the configuration of organizational fields: The IIRC and the pursuit of "Enlightened" corporate reporting. *Accounting and Business Research, 47*(1), 30–63. https://doi.org/10.1080/00014788.2016.1198683.

International Integrated Reporting Council (IIRC). (2013). *The international <IR> framework*. London: International Integrated Reporting Council. Available at: http://www.integratedreporting.org/wp-content/uploads/2015/03/13-12-08-THE-INTERNATIONAL-IR-FRAMEWORK-2-1.pdf. Accessed October 7, 2019.

Jönsson, S., & Lukka, K. (2005). *Doing interventionist research in management accounting*. Gothenburg: Gothenburg Research Institute.

La Torre, M., Dumay, J., Rea, M. A., & Abhayawansa, S. (2019). A "Journey" toward a safe harbor: The rhetorical process of the International Integrated Reporting Council. *The British Accounting Review (in press)*. https://doi.org/10.1016/j.bar.2019.100836.

Macias, H. A., & Farfan-Lievano, A. (2017). Integrated reporting as a strategy for firm growth: Multiple case study in Colombia. *Meditari Accountancy Research, 25*(4), 605–628. https://doi.org/10.1108/MEDAR-11-2016-0099.

McNally, M. A., Cerbone, D., & Maroun, W. (2017). Exploring the challenges of preparing an integrated report. *Meditari Accountancy Research, 25*(4), 481–504. https://doi.org/10.1108/MEDAR-10-2016-0085.

Milne, M. J., & Gray, R. (2013). W(h)ither ecology? The triple bottom line, the global reporting initiative, and corporate sustainability reporting. *Journal of Business Ethics, 118*(1), 13–29. https://doi.org/10.1007/s10551-012-1543-8.

Monciardini, D., Dumay, J. & Biondi, L. (2016). *Integrated reporting and EU law. Competing, converging or complementary regulatory frameworks?* Paper presented at the and EU Law. Competing, Converging or Complementary Regulatory Frameworks?—Life-cycle based management and reporting for sustainable business. 29–30 November 2016, Oslo, Norway.

Mouritsen, J. (2006). Problematising intellectual capital research: Ostensive versus performative IC. *Accounting, Auditing and Accountability Journal, 19*(6), 820–841. https://doi.org/10.1108/09513570610709881.

Petty, R., & Guthrie, J. (2000). Intellectual capital literature review: Measurement, reporting and management. *Journal of Intellectual Capital, 1*(2), 155–176. https://doi.org/10.1108/14691930010348731.

Rinaldi, L., Unerman, J., & de Villiers, C. (2018). Evaluating the Integrated Reporting journey: Insights, gaps and agendas for future research. *Accounting, Auditing and Accountability Journal, 31*(5), 1294–1318. https://doi.org/10.1108/AAAJ-04-2018-3446.

Rowbottom, N., & Locke, J. (2016). The emergence of <IR>. *Accounting and Business Research, 46*(1), 83–115. https://doi.org/10.1080/00014788.2015.1029867.

Sabelfeld, S. & Dumay, J. (2018). *Adoption of Integrated Reporting: Lost in local translation?* Financial Reporting Workshop, 14–15 June 2018, University of Bologna.

Stewart, T. A. (1991). Brainpower. *Fortune, 123*, 44–50.

Sveiby, K. E. (1989). *The invisible balance sheet: Key indicators for accounting, control and valuation of know-how companies (translation)*. The Konrad Group: Stockholm.

Thomson, I. (2015). 'But does sustainability need capitalism or an integrated report' a commentary on 'the international integrated reporting council: A story of failure' by Flower, J. *Critical Perspectives on Accounting, 27*, 18–22. https://doi.org/10.1016/j.cpa.2014.07.003.

Tucker, B. P., & Lowe, A. D. (2014). Practitioners are from Mars; academics are from Venus? An investigation of the research-practice gap in management accounting. *Accounting, Auditing and Accountability Journal, 27*(3), 394–425. https://doi.org/10.1108/AAAJ-01-2012-00932.

van Bommel, K. (2014). Towards a legitimate compromise? An exploration of integrated reporting in the Netherlands. *Accounting, Auditing and Accountability Journal, 27*(7), 1157–1189. https://doi.org/10.1108/AAAJ-04-2013-1309.

Chapter 4
Leonardo: All that Glitters Is not Gold

Abstract Given that <IR> is a relatively recent phenomenon, insights are needed to understand how it works in practice and, as a consequence, to ascertain if it could eventually become the corporate reporting norm as advocated by the IIRC. Adams (2015, p. 23) encourages "academics to engage with the [<IR>] process and to contribute to the development of new forms of accountings to help ensure [the <IR> Framework's] potential is reached". In response, this and the following chapter seek to provide insights into two organisations that have embarked on the journey towards <IR>. The two case studies contribute to the ongoing debate on <IR> by providing examples of how, and for what reasons, <IR> becomes part of a wider reporting eco-system and the conditions needed for its success (or lack thereof). To date, <IR> research has mainly adopted a top-down ostensive approach rather than a critical bottom-up performative stance based upon its implementation. Therefore, the case studies presented here seek to showcase how two different organisations attempted to operationalise <IR> and the journeys they went through to get there, as well as to derive insights into what new issues will potentially impact on <IR> practice in the future. The first case study delivers insights into a former subsidiary of the Finmeccanica Group that attempted to innovate its strategic management reporting system by moving from IC reporting to integrated thinking, and subsequently helping its holding company adopt <IR>. Following a major company restructure on 1 January 2016, the subsidiary is now one of five divisions of Leonardo S.p.A., a high-tech multinational company operating in the aerospace, defence, and security sector headquartered in Italy. The five divisions comprise helicopters, aircraft, aerostructures, electronics, and cybersecurity. Access to the data about the subsidiary's integrated thinking and reporting journey was given on the proviso of anonymity. Therefore, it has been given the fictional name Omega.

4.1 Omega's Profile

Omega is an international leader in electronics and information technology that designs and develops large systems for homeland protection, radar, and air and airport traffic management. Omega was its own legal entity until 31 December 2015

C. Bernardi, *Implementing Integrated Reporting*, SpringerBriefs in Accounting,
https://doi.org/10.1007/978-3-030-11193-9_4

and currently, as one of five divisions of Leonardo S.p.A., it operates in a discrete business sector. In accordance with the practices of Leonardo (the Finmeccanica Group at the time), Omega is fully committed to implementing policies for sustainability, transparency, and social responsibility that reflect the core values behind organisational activities (i.e., innovation, integrity, respect, customer intimacy, and people excellence). The company pursues its social responsibility by attempting to contribute to the well-being and growth of the communities in which it operates, not only from an economic point of view but also through social initiatives. To this end, it actively promotes strategies for sustainably managing the environment and for its employees' welfare and security. Additionally, Omega seeks to encourage people to develop to their full potential by promoting the highest standards of integrity, cultural excellence, and merit. Thus, Omega is, arguably, a good example of a company developing its sustainability agenda.

4.2 Motivations Behind Omega's Project

Omega's journey towards integrated thinking and reporting began as an experiment at the suggestion of the CEO to increase the company's IC. At the time the project started in 2010, the management at Omega wanted to explain their value creation goals from a more holistic perspective. They recognised that their disclosures should include both tangible and intangible assets. The motivation behind these disclosures was the increasing complexity of global competitive dynamics and the transition to a knowledge-based economy, defined by the OECD (1996, p. 7) as an economy "directly based on the production, distribution and use of knowledge and information". Management recognised that a knowledge-based economy meant they could no longer rely exclusively on tangible assets as long-term growth catalysts. Against this background, the company's intangible resources and capabilities progressively took on a preeminent role, and IC was increasingly acknowledged as an influential source of value creation and competitive advantage (Edvinsson and Malone 1997; Sveiby 1997).

Within this context, the Omega CEO was interested in unlocking and leveraging the company's IC. The expected output was a report to support managerial decision-making processes. Following changes in the parent company's top management and its inclusion in the Dow Jones Sustainability Index (DJSI), however, Omega chose to reinforce its commitment to sustainability, and this became the project's primary strategic objective, supplanting IC reporting. Thus, while Omega was originally motivated to integrate IC into its management practices, it later integrated sustainability into its business processes to align with the holding company strategy in order to measure, whenever possible, the value it created from a broader economic, social, and environmental stance.

4.3 The Project Team

Omega's journey began with an IC reporting and research project in 2010 that was scheduled to end in 2013. Initially, the project team was made up of three academic researchers and three project controllers from Omega. I became involved in 2012 as a fourth academic researcher. By 2013, the information system design was complete, but the project was never implemented as the following events will reveal. The project controllers were from the organisational unit in Omega responsible for fostering strategic intangible resources—specifically, promoting product innovation, increasing patents and trademarks, strengthening personnel competencies, and establishing and maintaining academic and industrial relationships. They were the project's sponsors and the 'gatekeepers' between the academics and the rest of Omega. These project controllers helped us become insiders—i.e., helped us to take part in the everyday processes and activities of the unit and work to "develop participatory interactions more akin to the interventionist process required for the conduct of interventionist research" (Dumay 2010, p. 55). Both groups shared the responsibility of delivering the project's output, but the controllers' commitment to a successful outcome went beyond a mere job requirement. They wanted to acquire new knowledge that would improve their competencies as controllers.

The following sections describe Omega and its business operations in more detail, plus how and why Omega was looking to develop its IC practices and a corresponding internal reporting system; the design of that system; and how the reporting project gradually evolved into one that integrated sustainability measures.

4.3.1 The Project Design

The project was conducted in light of *action research*, which traditionally involves " (…) a problem-solving relationship between researcher and client aimed at both solving a problem and generating new knowledge" (Coghlan and Brannick 2010, p. 44). This type of research is aimed at studying the resolution of organisational and social challenges with the people who have direct experience with those challenges. Such research methodology also involves observing processes and outcomes and analysing findings with the help of relevant literature.

The research project occurred in three distinct phases.

Phase I: Mapping Omega's IC

During Phase I, which lasted from 2010 to 2012, the project team aimed to design, develop, and implement an IC measurement system with the goal of publishing an internal IC report, which required data to measure. Some data was gathered from first-hand experience, but most data was also collected through interviews and reviews of internal documents. Between January 2010 and July 2012, the team attended 33 meetings each running four hours on average. Additionally, semi-structured interviews with the Chief Executive Officer and the Chief Financial Officer were recorded and transcribed along with field notes. The first phase of the project ended after two years and was validated by the CEO.

Phase II: Integrating IC within sustainability categories

In Phase II, which lasted from late 2012 to the end of 2013, the functionality of the model outlined for measuring, reporting, and managing IC was broadened to take sustainability into account. This was due to the fact that, shortly after launch, there were changes in the Finmeccanica Group's top management team and the company was included in the DJSI. As a result, sustainability became a primary strategic objective for both Omega and its parent company. Consequently, at the end of 2012 Omega's management decided to align its IC vision with the sustainability categories as envisaged by the holding company's strategy. To this end, they issued a master plan to implement specific sustainability initiatives while looking for a financial rationale to justify their decision. Part of the rationale came in the form of adding the main intangibles monitored by the DJSI (RobecoSAM 2013)[1] to the reporting scheme. Previously, these had not been considered as IC had been the focus. Each sustainability project underwent measurement, evaluation, and reporting, albeit through an IC lens, and the traditional vision of IC was used to incorporate sustainability concerns into three main capitals: structural, human, and relational.

During this phase, the joint research team was in charge of designing a specific monitoring system and then appointed to test it on the initiatives, which were planned to launch in 2014. The researchers intervened by collecting and reviewing internal documents and conducted semi-structured interviews with the company's management (i.e., Chief Financial Officer and Patent Manager) and the employees in charge of developing the social and environmental initiatives. These interviews were recorded and transcribed, along with field notes, to integrate the aforementioned company's IC mapping within the Finmeccanica's sustainability categories. The joint research team attended 24 meetings, each lasting an average of four hours. Further, the researchers conducted an accurate a literature review to find suggestions to integrate sustainability and IC issues.

Specifically, the activities involved:

i. Identifying the main initiatives that had a significant impact on IC, including aspects of sustainability and analysing their expected benefits;
ii. Measuring IC against various performance indicators, which included identifying relevant and strategic resources that could be reinforced and/or acquired by developing specific initiatives (again, including sustainability);
iii. Implementing initiatives and gathering data; and
iv. Assembling a report containing the results of the assessment for submission to the firm's top management at the end of the year (Fig. 4.1).

Phase III: Embarking on the journey towards <IR>

Although the design of the monitoring system was considered a managerial innovation for the company, the top managers decided not to go ahead with the implementation phase, which was scheduled for 2014. Phase III of the project did not involve

[1] http://www.robecosam.com. Accessed September 17, 2019.

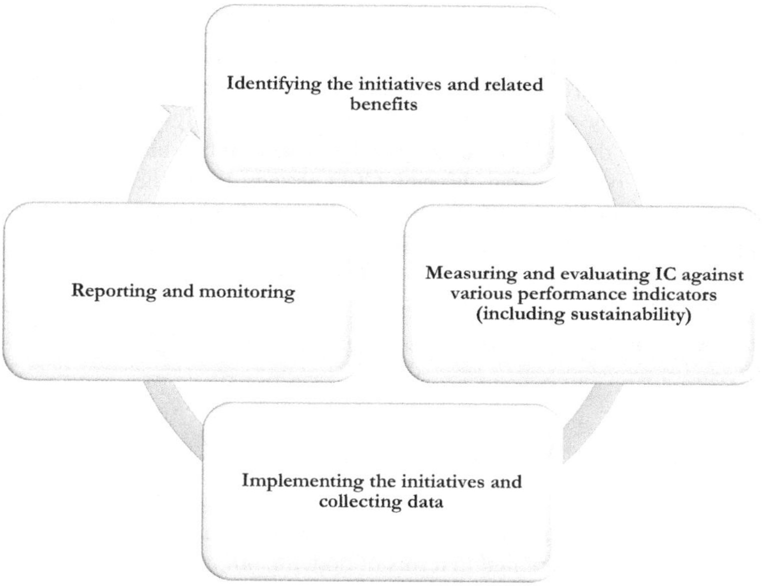

Fig. 4.1 Mapping and measuring sustainability at Omega

a physical presence at Omega for the researchers. However, researchers were keen to understand why the new monitoring system was not implemented and also to assess the overall project impact. Because Phase III was never implemented, we did not have the opportunity to test the new monitoring system; however, we could speculate on why, observed by us during the case, the company's management was interested in a tailored-made IC/sustainability measurement and reporting system and what subsequently led to abandoning Phase III.

Information about the events taking place was conveyed by one of the project controllers to the lead researcher. From 2014 to 2017, five semi-structured interviews with the former 'go-to' person were recorded, transcribed, and analysed with the aim to gather information on the organisational changes that occurred in the company and on the impact the research project had in terms of knowledge transfer for individuals and the organisation. The conclusion we reached is that the role of a visionary leader is fundamental for the diffusion of a new managerial culture like the one proposed. When the CEO resigned, the project was abandoned as it had not yet obtained widespread legitimacy. However, the transfer of mutual knowledge between researchers and professionals had taken hold and has become part of the skillset that individuals have been able to use in different contexts and organisational positions.

What the case demonstrates is that Omega was moving in the direction of integrated thinking and was only a short step from producing its own form of integrated reporting when the journey was halted because the CEO who initiated the project resigned. By contrast, the new CEO showed no interest in continuing the journey and terminated the project. A few years later, the Finmeccanica Group merged into one company, Leonardo S.p.A., who undertook its own experiments with <IR>. One can speculate two possible reasons for the new Omega CEO's lack of interest in continuing the integrated reporting journey. First is that these types of internal reporting/management control systems, which are arguably consistent with integrated thinking, are doomed if the top management is antagonistic to the initiative. Alternatively, it is possible that the new CEO already knew the holding company was going to engage with an <IR> project (as discussed in the next sections), and the Omega project was terminated due to potential overlaps or redundancy. Arguably, the journey towards integrated thinking and integrated reporting that happened at a subsidiary/divisional level took its own path and is only part of the story of what drives the corporate reporting journey at Leonardo S.p.A.

4.4 Leonardo S.p.A.: An Overview

The aerospace, defence, and security industry comprises mainly multinational companies that are highly diversified in terms of both the products they manufacture and their geographical location. Overall, the rivalry within this sector is strong. Given that the degree of specialisation is very high, expertise and knowledge are crucial determinants of a firm's success. Moreover, companies operating in this sector are compelled to adhere to strict regulations, including national security, export restrictions, licensing, accounting rules, and safety requirements. Due to the increasing level of competition in innovation and new technology, firms need to constantly increase their intangible resources, their efficiency, and their effectiveness.

Leonardo is a volatile enterprise that is at the mercy of politics and global instability. Due to turmoil in some of its key markets, it has a chequered financial performance (see Fig. 4.2). Political pressures, emerging conflicts, and various vicissitudes associated with changes to international regimes and governments have resulted in several major changes in its relationships with key customers that have impacted its financial success. The worst year was 2011 when the Finmeccanica Group declared a 22% decrease in new orders and a €2.3 billion loss. These losses came as the result of an organisational restructure that saw a significant decrease in non-recurring income, restructuring costs, and the impairment of goodwill when it divested from several non-performing businesses. As the then Chairman and CEO, Giuseppe Orsi, admitted in the 2011 Annual Report:

> *Dear shareholders and stakeholders, during the lifespan of a company, it is necessary to regularly "take stock" of the situation: examine the operating conditions, the effectiveness of the decisions made, the accuracy of the strategies outlined, and finally, the correspondence of the path followed to the intended objectives. This is important, not only to highlight possible wrong turns that may need correcting, but also and above all to take into account the gap between the operational conditions initially expected, and those that, due to factors outside the company's control, actually occurred. (Annual Report* 2011*, p. 8)*

During the period from 2011 to 2013, Finmeccanica became embroiled in scandals as part of WikiLeaks that eventually led to changes in management. Most notable

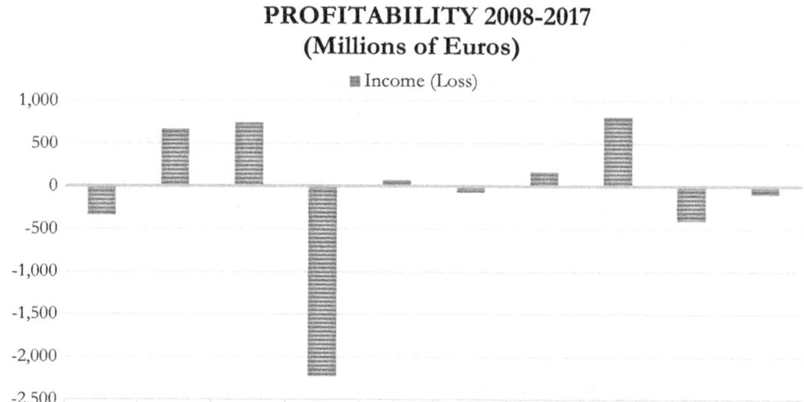

	2008	2009	2010	2011	2012	2013	2014	2015	2016	2017
Income (Loss)	-335	671	741	-2221	74	-67	172	816	-399	-90

Fig. 4.2 The changing fortunes of Leonardo S.p.A.

was the sale of mobile telecommunications equipment to Syria in 2011 after the start of the Syrian uprising. Additionally, in 2013, the CEO was arrested on charges of corruption and bribery to secure the sale of helicopters to India.

The company's overall performance improved in 2012, but the company was still under pressure in several core markets and new orders continued to decrease, although not as significantly as in 2011. The new CEO, Alessandro Pansa, appointed after Orsi's arrest, helped to stabilise the business but did not manage a substantial improvement in profitability.

2014 saw the appointment of yet another CEO, Mauro Moretti, who embarked on significant changes and divestments from some of the non-core businesses. By 2015, the company appeared to have rebounded, showing its best financial performance since 2010. Unfortunately, the prosperity was short-lived, reversing in 2016. The continued challenging operating environment in 2017 and pressure from the Italian Government, saw the appointment of the fourth and current CEO, Alessandro Profumo, who is undertaking profound changes in the company as he drives for new efficiencies as part of a novel industrial plan stretching from 2018 to 2022. Thus, Leonardo has undergone several significant changes in strategy and leadership over the past decade, and this is reflected in its journey towards <IR> as revealed next.

4.4.1 The Journey Towards <IR> at Leonardo S.p.A.

As discussed in the previous chapter, it is important to understand that, when a company first issues an integrated report, it makes a conscious decision to incorporate the <IR> Framework in accordance with its reporting needs. Most importantly, there is no evidence to show that implementing <IR> is an action that then supersedes other reporting instruments, especially because most companies need to comply with regulated frameworks. They also need to demonstrate that they have complied with specific standards relating to their industry as well as issues like quality control and assurance. As such, for most companies, reporting requirements are a matrix of standards, regulatory instruments, and selected voluntary instruments. <IR> does not occur in a vacuum but, rather more realistically, within a corporate reporting and disclosure eco-system. Table 4.1[2] presents an analysis of that eco-system, followed by a discussion. More details on the different reporting frameworks and standards listed in the table are provided in the Appendix.

4.4.2 The EU Directive

As Leonardo discloses in its 2017 Annual Financial Report, implementing <IR> was partially in response to complying with the EU Directive (Directive 2014/95/EU) on non-financial reporting, which also incorporates compliance with the GRI:

> *The approach to Sustainability, as well as any action and initiative taken during the year, are described in the Sustainability and Innovation Report 2017, which also constitutes a nonfinancial Declaration pursuant to Legislative Decree 254 of 30 December 2016 and which is prepared on an annual basis, according to the guidelines of the Global Reporting Initiative (GRI) and of the framework of the International Integrated Reporting Council (IIRC) and assured by KPMG. (Annual Financial Report* 2017a, *p. 69)*

Thus, it is evident that <IR> was to be an important new aspect of Leonardo's reporting and, more specifically, its drive to report on innovation and sustainability rather than being directly linked to the company's annual financial reporting requirements. However, while integrated reporting is mentioned in the annual report, it is only ever applied in the *Sustainability and Innovation Report*. Moreover, <IR> is not the report's primary framework: the requirements of the recent EU Directive appear to have usurped the structure, as explained in the Introduction (Annual Financial Report 2017a):

> *Leonardo is subject to the Italian Legislative Decree no. 254/2016, transposing the Directive 2014/95/EU of the European Parliament on the disclosure of non-financial information.*

In accordance with the law, Leonardo had prepared a separate and consolidated non-financial statement, called the *Sustainability and Innovation Report 2017*, designed to communicate the company's idea of sustainability and long-term approach to value creation to its stakeholders:

---

[2]Leonardo's reports between 2009 and 2017 were imported into NVivo. Any frameworks or standards mentioned were identified from a full manual reading. A follow-up search for key terms, such as ISO, GRI, integrated report, Global Compact, and EU Directive, in both Italian and English was used to confirm every mention had been identified.

Table 4.1 Leonardo's corporate reporting and disclosure eco-system

Year	2009	2010		2011		2012		2013		2014		2015		2016		2017	
Reporting instrument or standard	AR	AR	SR	AR	SR	AR	SR	AR	SR	AR	SR	AR	SIR	AR	SIR	AR	SIR
Early reporting instruments or standards																	
Global Reporting Initiative (GRI)		x	x	x	x	x	x	x	x	x	x	x	x	x	x	x	x
Corporate Governance	x	x	x	x	x	x	x	x	x	x	x	x	x	x	x	x	x
Code of Ethics	x	x	x	x	x	x	x	x	x	x	x	x	x	x	x	x	x
Anti-Corruption Code											x		x	x	x		x
Corporate Governance Report	x	x	x	x	x	x	x	x	x	x	x		x		x		x
United Nations (UN) Global Compact					x		x		x		x						
Recent instruments or standards																	
Integrated Reporting (<IR>)																x	x
Legislative Decree 254															x	x	x
United Nations Sustainable Development Goals (UNSDGs)															x	x	x
Task Force on Climate-Related Financial Disclosures (TCFD)																	x
Other underlying standards																	
SA8000® Standard			x	x					x		x		x		x		
ISO 14001—Environmental management	x	x	x	x	x		x		x	x	x	x	x	x	x	x	x
ISO 50001—Energy management						x	x		x		x		x		x		x

Legend AR—Annual Report; SR—Sustainability Report; SIR—Sustainability and Innovation Report

> *In this way, we aim to valorise the path undertaken by the Group over the last years and to interpret the constructive spirit of the Directive, whose purpose is to increase the comprehension and the level of disclosure of the non-financial information. (Sustainability and Innovation Report* 2017b, *p. 5)*

The document is ostensibly drawn up according to the GRI's "G4—Sustainability Reporting Guidelines" with the option "In accordance: Core" (a bridging table in the Appendix indicates the contents required by the Legislative Decree No. 254/2016). However, the *Sustainability and Innovation Report* is oddly inspired by the <IR> Framework.

Oddly because, in the report, <IR> is like the new kid on the block making claims about becoming the next corporate reporting norm. On the one hand, the report is one of the few that outlines the alignment between complying with new EU/Italian regulations while voluntarily adopting aspects of the GRI and <IR>. On the other, the report makes it apparent that frameworks are being cherry-picked. In fact, this GRI/<IR>-based report is only one among many other reports published to show that Leonardo is complying with its regulatory responsibilities. Its annual financial report, a code of ethics, an anti-corruption code, and a corporate governance report are all offered as documents in support of compliance.

Nor are these new disclosures for Leonardo. With the exception of its anti-corruption code, all the documents listed under the *Italian Legislative Decree 254* have been an essential part of Leonardo's reporting since 2010. Thus, complying with the *Italian Legislative Decree 254* appears to have been a relatively easy reorganisation of its disclosures. Arguably, for a company like Leonardo, this does not constitute a dramatic change in corporate reporting.

The difference between complying with the *Italian Legislative Decree 254* and implementing <IR> is that there are no real requirements or boxes to tick with <IR>. While the <IR> Framework has a structure, there is no penalty for non-compliance, and the <IR>'s Framework is ambiguous enough to allow companies to report what they want according to their own needs (Dumay et al. 2017). Therefore, for Leonardo, <IR> has become a part of complying with the *Italian Legislative Decree 254* rather than complying with a framework that results in a meaningful integrated report.

4.4.3 Other Reporting Frameworks

What is also interesting about Table 4.1 is the evidence of the different reporting frameworks used by Leonardo as part of its corporate reporting journey over the years. For example, GRI is used consistently across the period (starting in 2010), whereas the UN Global Compact is only referenced between 2011 and 2014. So, while <IR> is the new kid on the block, other voluntary reporting frameworks also appear around the same time—most notably, the United Nations Sustainable Development Goals (UNSDGs) (2016–2017) and disclosures relating to the Task Force on Climate-Related Financial Disclosures (TCFD) (2017).

These two topics are equally hot in corporate disclosure and reporting research today. Many companies are now making disclosures related to the UNSDGs, and early evidence suggests that these disclosures will outpace, or have already outpaced, reports based on <IR>. According to the Sustainable Development Goals (SDGs) Reporting Challenge 2018 by PWC (2018):

- Every organisation is influenced by or operationalise meeting the SDGs.
- The SDGs have broken into the mainstream of business reporting:
  - 72% now mention the goals in their annual corporate or sustainability report
  - 50% of companies have identified priority SDGs.

Refusing to give up the fight, the IIRC is also advocating that companies incorporate the UNSDGs into their integrated reports (Adams 2017). However, <IR> already has an overly complex business model and linking the 17 UNSDGs with the six capitals and their interactions has only further exacerbated the problem. Leonardo has opted for a different approach with a separate one-page excerpt in its *Sustainability and Innovation Report* (2017b, p. 30) that lists and explains four UNSDGs as priorities (4—Quality education; 8—Decent work and economic growth; 9—Industry, innovation and infrastructure; and 13—Climate action). Thus, the UNSDGs are considered independently with no links to the <IR> business model.

Disclosures relating to the TCFD is another aspect of Leonardo's integrated reporting. Launched by the G20 Finance Ministers and Governors of the Central Banks, and driven by the Financial Stability Board, Leonardo joined the TCFD in 2017, thus committing itself to voluntary disclosures about the risks and opportunities associated with climate change. Again, there is no clear link to the <IR> Framework, its business model, or its capitals in the text. However, there are specific links to the metrics recommended by the GRI.

4.4.4 Other Underlying Standards

Investigating the reasons for why all these frameworks have been used is not the intention here. Nevertheless, it is important to highlight that Leonardo does report on its activities and is compliant with several different international and industry standards, such as ISO 14001—Environmental management, ISO 50001—Energy management and SA8000® Standard—Socially responsible employment practice. While these standards do not constitute reporting frameworks, they are an equally important part of Leonardo's reporting journey because they are evidence that the company complies with social initiatives in environment, energy, labour, and so forth. Arguably, Leonardo walks the talk. Additionally, complying with a number of different standards shows that Leonardo is committed to developing systems to assure management and its stakeholders that it is fully committed to action and not just reporting.

4.5 The Future of <IR> at Leonardo

It will be interesting to see how Leonardo's reporting journey evolves, both internally and externally, as not all of its previous subsidiaries have experience with integrated thinking and reporting like Omega did. Given that Leonardo only drew up its first <IR>-inspired *Sustainability and Innovation Report* in 2017, it is reasonable to claim that the company's journey towards <IR> is still in its initial stages.

On these grounds, I would argue that Leonardo's integrated thinking is not currently firmly embedded in the company's management processes. I also contend that the case evidence suggests Leonardo will have difficulty in quickly producing an effective integrated report that reflects a business model which explicitly takes the <IR> Framework into account. The reasoning behind my conclusion is a shared and pervasive form of management control called "tone at the top", which is a crucial and necessary enabler of <IR> if it has any chance of being implemented successfully (Dumay and Dai 2017).

Putting aside the likelihood of success of Leonardo's experiment with <IR>, I put forward an aside as to why it might have engaged with <IR> in the first place, noting that these reasons are not entirely clear, given that the researchers currently have no direct access to the company and its recent dynamics. It can be speculated, however, that one possible reason is organisational legitimacy (Suchman 1995). The reasons behind changes in internal policy may be associated with the necessity to maintain a certain company profile capable of positively impressing stakeholders, who may influence the independent choice of the management in terms of the measures to be adopted. It can be argued that the adoption of <IR> is a "structurally determined" mechanism to "strategically respond" to the pressures of the external environment. Therefore, it is possible that Leonardo is acting in line with Dumay et al.'s (2015, p. 2) definition of "material legitimacy", defined as "the form of legitimacy that enables organisations to blend what is important to the organisation (strategic legitimacy) with the primary concerns of its major stakeholders (institutional legitimacy)". In this sense, companies try to achieve positive internal and external outcomes by making useful decisions that are internally consistent with their overall strategy and that are also externally pleasing to stakeholders. There is, however, an inherent difficulty in separating externally and internally driven policies, as often decisions are a form of 'golden mean' intended to strike a balance between the different forces at play.

Appendix: Frameworks and Descriptions

Framework name, host organisation, and URL	A brief description from their website
Legislative Decree 254 (Directive 2015/94/EU) Commissione Nazionale per le Società e la Borsa—known as CONSOB to transpose the Directive of the European Commission into Italian Law http://www.consob.it/web/consob-and-its-activities/laws-and-regulations/documenti/english/laws/reg20267e.pdf	The regulation that implemented Legislative Decree 254 of December 30, 2016, which relates to reporting non-financial information. The regulation is in support of EU Directive 2015/94/EU as amended by the European Parliament in 2014. The Directive's purpose is as follows: In its resolutions of 6 February 2013 on, 'Corporate Social Responsibility: Accountable, transparent and responsible business behaviour and sustainable growth' and 'Corporate Social Responsibility: Promoting society's interests and a route to sustainable and inclusive recovery', the European Parliament acknowledged that it is important for businesses that wish to identify sustainability risks and increase investor and consumer trust to release information on sustainability, such as social and environmental factors. Disclosing non-financial information is vital for managing change towards a sustainable global economy by combining long-term profitability with social justice and environmental protection. In this context, disclosing non-financial information helps to measure, monitor, and manage the performance of undertakings and their impact on society. Thus, the European Parliament called on the Commission to bring forward a legislative proposal on the disclosure of non-financial information by undertakings. This proposal allows actions to be highly flexible to account for the multidimensional nature of corporate social responsibility (CSR) and the diversity of the CSR policies implemented by businesses. These actions are matched by a sufficient level of comparability to meet the needs of investors and other stakeholders, as well as the need to provide consumers with easy access to information on how businesses impact society.
International <IR> Framework International Integrated Reporting Council http://integratedreporting.org/resource/international-ir-framework/	<IR> applies principles and concepts that are focused on bringing greater cohesion and efficiency to the reporting process and adopting 'integrated thinking' as a way of breaking down internal silos and reducing duplication. It improves the quality of information available to providers of financial capital to enable a more efficient and productive allocation of capital. Its focus on value creation, and the 'capitals' used by the business to create value over time, contributes towards a more financially stable global economy.
United Nations Sustainable Development Goals United Nations https://www.un.org/sustainabledevelopment/sustainable-development-goals/	The Sustainable Development Goals are the blueprint for achieving a better and more sustainable future for all. They address the global challenges we face, including those related to poverty, inequality, climate, environmental degradation, prosperity, and peace and justice. The Goals interconnect and, to leave no one behind, it is important that we achieve each Goal and target by 2030.

(continued)

(continued)

Framework name, host organisation, and URL	A brief description from their website
Task Force on Climate-Related Financial Disclosures (TCFD) Financial Stability Board https://www.fsb-tcfd.org/	The FSB Task Force on Climate-Related Financial Disclosures (TCFD) will develop voluntary, consistent climate-related financial risk disclosures for use by companies in providing information to investors, lenders, insurers, and other stakeholders. The Task Force will consider the physical, liability, and transition risks associated with climate change and what constitutes effective financial disclosures across industries. The work and recommendations of the Task Force will help companies understand what financial markets want from disclosures to measure and respond to climate change risks and encourage firms to align their disclosures with investors' needs.
Global Reporting Initiative (GRI) Global Reporting Initiative https://www.globalreporting.org/Pages/default.aspx	GRI helps businesses and governments worldwide understand and communicate their impact on critical sustainability issues, such as climate change, human rights, governance, and social well-being. This enables real action to create social, environmental, and economic benefits for everyone. The GRI Sustainability Reporting Standards are developed with true multi-stakeholder contributions and rooted in the public interest.

(continued)

(continued)

Framework name, host organisation, and URL	A brief description from their website
UN Global Compact United Nations https://www.unglobalcompact.org/	At the UN Global Compact, they aim to mobilise a global movement of sustainable companies and stakeholders to create the world they want. That is their vision. To make this happen, the UN Global Compact supports companies to: • Do business responsibly by aligning their strategies and operations with Ten Principles on human rights, labour, environment, and anti-corruption; and • Take strategic actions to advance broader societal goals, such as the UN Sustainable Development Goals, with an emphasis on collaboration and innovation. **The Ten Principles of the UN Global Compact** Corporate sustainability starts with a company's value system and a principles-based approach to doing business. This means operating in ways that, at a minimum, meet fundamental responsibilities in the areas of human rights, labour, environment, and anti-corruption. Responsible businesses enact the same values and principles wherever they have a presence and know that good practices in one area do not offset harm in another. By incorporating the Ten Principles of the UN Global Compact into strategies, policies, and procedures, and establishing a culture of integrity, companies are not only upholding their basic responsibilities to the people and the planet but also setting the stage for long-term success. The Ten Principles of the United Nations Global Compact are derived from: • the Universal Declaration of Human Rights; • the International Labour Organization's Declaration on Fundamental Principles and Rights at Work; • the Rio Declaration on Environment and Development; and • the United Nations Convention Against Corruption. Human Rights Principle 1: Businesses should support and respect the protection of internationally proclaimed human rights; and Principle 2: Make sure that they are not complicit in human rights abuses. Labour Principle 3: Businesses should uphold the freedom of association and the effective recognition of the right to collective bargaining; Principle 4: The elimination of all forms of forced and compulsory labour; Principle 5: The effective abolition of child labour; and Principle 6: The elimination of discrimination in respect of employment and occupation. Environment Principle 7: Businesses should support a precautionary approach to environmental challenges; Principle 8: Undertake initiatives to promote greater environmental responsibility; and Principle 9: Encourage the development and diffusion of environmentally friendly technologies. Anti-Corruption Principle 10: Businesses should work against corruption in all its forms, including extortion and bribery.

(continued)

(continued)

Framework name, host organisation, and URL	A brief description from their website
Corporate Governance Various https://iclg.com/practice-areas/corporate-governance-laws-and-regulations/italy	The Italian Civil Code (ICC) is the main corporate governance source for any Italian company. Additionally, upon incorporation any company must adopt its by-laws, which set forth the main rules regarding, *inter alia*, the management body, its composition, its role, and its function. Listed companies are also subject to the following rules: Legislative Decree no. 58/1998 (Testo Unico della Finanza—TUF), regulatory provisions issued by the Commissione Nazionale per le Società e la Borsa—CONSOB (the Italian authority that is responsible for the supervision of the Italian securities market) or by Borsa Italiana S.p.A. (the company managing the Italian Stock Exchange), and related secondary regulations. Additionally, listed companies may voluntarily adopt a self-regulation Corporate Governance Code (the 'Code'), issued by the Corporate Governance Committee of Borsa Italiana S.p.A. The Code is based on the "comply or explain" principle: companies are free to decide whether to follow the recommendations or not. In case of any deviation they are required to give an explanation, for the benefit of shareholders, investors, and the market.
SA8000® Standard Social Accountability International http://www.sa-intl.org/index.cfm?fuseaction=Page.ViewPage&PageID=1689	The SA8000® Standard is the leading social certification standard for factories and organisations across the globe. It was established by Social Accountability International in 1997 as a multi-stakeholder initiative. Over the years, the Standard has evolved into an overall framework that helps certified organisations demonstrate their dedication to the fair treatment of workers across industries and in any country.
OHSAS 18001 British Standards Institution https://www.bsigroup.com/LocalFiles/en-AE/Risk/OHSAS%2018001/New%20Brochures/BS-OHSAS-18001-Implementation-Guide.pdf	OHSAS 1801:2007 Occupational Health and Safety Management Certification is an international standard that provides a framework to identify, control, and decrease the risks associated with health and safety within the workplace. Implementing the standard will send a clear signal to your stakeholders that you view employee's health and safety as a priority within your organisation.
ISO 14001—Environmental management International Organization for Standardization https://www.iso.org/iso-14001-environmental-management.html	The ISO 14000 family of standards provides practical tools for companies and organisations of all kinds looking to manage their environmental responsibilities. ISO 14001:2015 and its supporting standards, such as ISO 14006:2011, focus on environmental systems. The other standards in the family focus on specific approaches, such as audits, communications, labelling, and life cycle analysis, as well as environmental challenges like climate change.

(continued)

(continued)

Framework name, host organisation, and URL	A brief description from their website
ISO 50001—Energy management International Organization for Standardization https://www.iso.org/iso-50001-energy-management.html	Using energy efficiently helps organisations save money as well as conserve resources and tackle climate change. ISO 50001 supports organisations in all sectors to use energy more efficiently, through the development of an energy management system (EnMS). ISO 50001 is based on the management system model of continual improvement also used for other well-known standards, such as ISO 9001 or ISO 14001. This makes it easier for organisations to integrate energy management into their overall efforts to improve quality and environmental management. ISO 50001:2018 provides a framework of requirements for organisations to: • Develop a policy for a more efficient use of energy; • Fix targets and objectives to meet the policy; • Use data to better understand and make decisions about energy use; • Measure the results; • Review how well the policy works; and • Continually improve energy management.
ISO 9000 family—Quality management International Organization for Standardization https://www.iso.org/iso-9001-quality-management.html	The ISO 9000 family addresses various aspects of quality management and contains some of ISO's best-known standards. The standards provide guidance and tools for companies and organisations who want to ensure that their products and services consistently meet customer requirements and that quality is consistently improved. ISO 9001:2015 sets out the criteria for a quality management system and is the only standard in the family that provides certification (although this is not a requirement). It can be used by any organisation, large or small, regardless of its field of activity. In fact, there are over one million companies and organisations in over 170 countries that are ISO 9001 certified.
International Petroleum Industry Environmental Conservation Association (IPIECA) IPIECA http://www.ipieca.org/about-us/	IPIECA develops, shares, and promotes good practice and knowledge to help industry and improve environmental and social performance. It does this with the understanding that the issues that dominate the sustainable development agenda—climate and energy, environmental and social issues—are too big for individual companies to tackle alone. Industry must work together to achieve improvements that have real impact. IPIECA helps to achieve this goal. IPIECA is a not for profit association that provides a forum for encouraging continuous improvement in industry performance. It is the only global association involving both the upstream and downstream oil and gas industry. It is also the industry's principal channel of communication with the United Nations.

(continued)

(continued)

Framework name, host organisation, and URL	A brief description from their website
Dow Jones Sustainability World Indices RobecoSAM https://www.sustainability-indices.com/	The Dow Jones Sustainability Indices were launched in 1999 as the first global sustainability benchmarks. The indices are offered cooperatively by RobecoSAM and S&P Dow Jones Indices. The family tracks the stock performance of the world's leading companies in terms of economic, environmental, and social criteria. The indices serve as benchmarks for investors who integrate sustainability considerations into their portfolios and provide an effective engagement platform for companies who want to adopt sustainable best practices.
FTSE4Good FTSE Russel (London Stock Exchange Group) https://www.ftse.com/products/indices/ftse4good	The FTSE4Good Index Series is designed to measure the performance of companies demonstrating strong environmental, social, and governance (ESG) practices. Transparent management and clearly-defined ESG criteria make FTSE4Good indices suitable tools to be used by a wide variety of market participants when creating or assessing sustainable investment products. FTSE4Good indexes can be used in four main ways: • Financial products—As tools in the creation of index-tracking investments, financial instruments, or fund products focused on sustainable investment. • Research—To identify environmentally and socially sustainable companies; • Reference—As a transparent and evolving global ESG standard that companies can assess their progress and achievements against; and • Benchmarking—As a benchmark index to track the performance of sustainable investment portfolios.

References

Adams, C. A. (2015). The international integrated reporting council: A call to action. *Critical Perspectives on Accounting, 27*, 23–28. https://doi.org/10.1016/j.cpa.2014.07.001.

Adams, C. (2017). *The sustainable development goals, integrated thinking and the integrated report*. London: International Integrated Reporting Council. Available at: https://integratedreporting.org/resource/sdgs-integrated-thinking-and-the-integrated-report/. Accessed September 8, 2019.

Coghlan, D., & Brannick, T. (2010). *Doing action research in your own organization* (3rd ed.). London: Sage.

Dumay, J. (2010). A critical reflective discourse of an interventionist research project. *Qualitative Research in Accounting and Management, 7*(1), 46–70. https://doi.org/10.1108/11766091011034271.

Dumay, J., & Dai, T. (2017). Integrated thinking as a cultural control? *Meditari Accountancy Research, 25*(4), 574–604. https://doi.org/10.1108/MEDAR-07-2016-0067.

Dumay, J., Bernardi, C., Guthrie, J., & La Torre, M. (2017). Barriers to implementing the international integrated reporting framework: A contemporary academic perspective. *Meditari Accountancy Research, 25*(4), 461–480. https://doi.org/10.1108/MEDAR-05-2017-0150.

Dumay, J., Frost, G., & Beck, C. (2015). Material legitimacy: Blending organisational and stakeholder concerns through non-financial information disclosures. *Journal of Accounting & Organizational Change, 11*(1), 2–23. https://doi.org/10.1108/JAOC-06-2013-0057.

Edvinsson, L., & Malone, S. (1997). *Intellectual capital: Realizing your company's true value by finding its hidden brainpower*. New York: Harper Collins.

European Union. (2014). *Directive 2014/95/EU of the European Parliament and of the Council*. Available at: https://eur-lex.europa.eu/legal-content/EN/TXT/?uri=CELEX%3A32014L0095.

Finmeccanica. (2011). *Finmeccanica annual report*. Available at: https://www.leonardocompany.com/investors/results-and-reports. Accessed September 25, 2019.

Leonardo. (2017a). *Annual financial report*. Available at: https://www.leonardocompany.com/investors/results-and-reports. Accessed August 29, 2019.

Leonardo. (2017b). *2017 sustainability and innovation report*. Available at: https://www.leonardocompany.com/en/about-us/sustainability/approach-and-reporting/reporting. Accessed August 30, 2019.

Organisation for Economic Co-operation and Development (OECD). (1996). *The knowledge-based economy*. Paris. Available at: http://www.oecd.org/officialdocuments/publicdisplaydocumentpdf/?cote=OCDE/GD%2896%29102&docLanguage=En. Accessed November 13, 2019.

PricewaterhouseCoopers (PWC). (2018). *SDG reporting challenge*. Available at: www.pwc.com/sdgreportingchallenge. Accessed September 6, 2019.

Suchman, M. C. (1995). Managing legitimacy: Strategic and institutional approaches. *The Academy of Management Review, 20*(3), 571–610. https://doi.org/10.2307/258788.

Sveiby, K. E. (1997). *The new organizational wealth: Managing and measuring knowledge-based assets*. San Francisco, CA: Berrett-Koehler.

Chapter 5
Eni: The Midas Touch

Abstract This chapter provides insights into the <IR> journey taken by Eni S.p.A., a multinational company operating in the oil and gas industry. Eni's claim of commitment to sustainability is proven by achievements and awards and, more importantly, its history. This case study, which is based on data and information gathered from different sources, including interviews, reveals a company that is seemingly making a genuine effort to improve its corporate reporting practices without any external obligation. Rather, it has an eye to new emerging reporting frameworks that fit with changing social, environmental and business contexts. In this vein, <IR> is used in complement with other reporting models to communicate appropriately with different audiences. The conclusions drawn contribute to third-stage performative <IR> research by delivering insights into the dynamics through which <IR> has evolved to become an established practice within a suite of reporting initiatives.

5.1 A Profile of Eni S.p.A.

Established by law as an Italian public entity in 1953, Eni is a large integrated energy company with a presence in 67 countries, nearly 32,000 employees worldwide, and a market capitalisation of approximately €50 billion (Eni Annual Report 2018). Its activities comprise oil and gas exploration, production, refining, and sales, plus power generation, chemicals, and plastics manufacturing. Until 1995, Eni operated as a nationalised company, after which it was privatised and almost 70% of its shares were floated. Since then, Eni's shares have been listed on both the FTSE/MIB Index[1] of the Italian Stock Exchange and the New York Stock Exchange.

In the decades following Eni's establishment, the company developed under the leadership of its chairman, Enrico Mattei. Mattei has long held a vision to pursue key international business alliances while, arguably, maintaining a strong commitment to its employees' well-being and to making a positive impact on society. For example, Eni's headquarters have, since the 1950s, contained a residential complex

[1]The basket including the 40 most traded stock classes listed on the Italian Stock Exchange.

C. Bernardi, *Implementing Integrated Reporting*, SpringerBriefs in Accounting,
https://doi.org/10.1007/978-3-030-11193-9_5

for its employees, plus a day-care centre, school, sports centre, and movie theatre. In tandem, Mattei's innovative program of international expansion, which has come to be known as the 'Mattei Formula', offers crude producer states an active and equal role in profiting from their natural resources.

Initially, Eni's expansion efforts focussed on North Africa with a signed exploration agreement with the Nasser-led Egyptian government dated December 1954. Similar joint ventures followed, and in March 1957 an agreement was signed with the Shah of Persia, Reza Phlevi, and the Iranian national oil company. During the years of the Cold War, Eni further established relationships and signed agreements with countries like the Soviet Union (1960), and also managed to play a mediating role in the dialogue between China and Russia, which was becoming increasingly complicated.

As a large multinational company with oil and gas interests, Eni is at risk of falling foul of the environmental and social concerns to which the industry is prone, e.g., pollution, exploitation, corruption, and so on. Identifying and mitigating the risks and hazards inherent to operating in this industry is likely a top-of-mind issue for Eni. In fact, Eni claims that sustainability has been imprinted in its genetic heritage since its origins, right alongside culture, partnership, innovation, and efficiency. Sustainability is one of its core values, described in its mission as follows:

> *We are an energy company. We are working to build a future where everyone can access energy resources efficiently and sustainably. Our work is based on passion and innovation, on our unique strengths and skills, on the quality of our people and in recognising that diversity across all aspects of our operations and organisation is something to be cherished. We believe in the value of long-term partnerships with the countries and communities where we operate. (Eni Integrated Annual Report* 2017d*)*

As with the Leonardo case study, the reporting frameworks and standards Eni uses can provide a deeper understanding of its journey towards <IR>. A summary of these (2006–2017) appears in Table 5.1.[2] Similar to Leonardo, Eni also 'walks the talk'. It complies with several different international and industry standards over labour, the environment, energy, quality, and so forth, each of which is integral to its operations and sustainability commitments. Even though Eni does not disclose as much about these standards as Leonardo does, merely mentioning these principles in a report shows evidence of the institutional pressure along with a desire to demonstrate Eni's compliance to stakeholders. Notably, over the years Eni has adhered to several initiatives and/or associations aimed at promoting sustainability-oriented practices, including the Business Council for Sustainable Development (BCSD 1990), the United Nations Global Compact (2001), the Global Gas Flaring Reduction (GGFR 2003) and the Extractive Industries Transparency Index (EITI 2005), and the International Petroleum Industry Environmental Conservation Association (IPIECA 2009).

The first explicit annual Sustainability Report produced by Eni dates back to 2006. The report was the result of a discussion process involving all corporate levels. The

[2]As in the case of Leonardo, the table was created by loading all the company's reports into NVivo. Any frameworks or standards mentioned were identified from a full manual reading. A follow-up search for key terms, such as ISO, GRI, integrated report, Global Compact, and EU Directive—both in Italian and English—was used to confirm every mention had been identified.

Table 5.1 Eni's corporate reporting and disclosure eco-system

Year	2006		2007		2008		2009		2010		2011		2012		2013		2014		2015		2016		2017	
Reporting instrument or standard	AR	SR	AR	SR	AR	SR	AR	SR	AR	SR	AR	EF	AR	EF	AR	EF	IR	EF	IR	EF	IR	EF	IR	EF
Early reporting instruments or standards																								
United Nations (UN) Global Compact	x	x		x		x	x	x	x	x	x	x	x	x	x	x	x	x	x	x	x	x	x	x
Global Reporting Initiative (GRI)		x		x		x		x		x		x	x	x	x	x	x	x	x	x		x	x	x
International Petroleum Industry Environmental Conservation Association (IPIECA)		x		x		x		x		x		x		x		x		x		x		x		x
Dow Jones Sustainability World Indexes		x		x		x		x				x		x										
FTSE4Good		x	x	x	x	x	x	x		x		x	x	x					x		x			
Corporate Governance	x	x	x	x	x	x	x	x	x	x	x	x	x		x	x	x	x	x	x	x	x	x	x
Code of Ethics			x	x	x	x	x	x	x	x	x	x	x	x	x	x	x	x	x	x	x	x	x	x
Anti-Corruption Policy							x			x	x	x												

(continued)

Table 5.1 (continued)

Year	2006		2007		2008		2009		2010		2011		2012		2013		2014		2015		2016		2017	
Reporting instrument or standard	AR	SR	AR	SR	AR	SR	AR	SR	AR	SR	AR	EF	AR	EF	AR	EF	IR	EF	IR	EF	IR	EF	IR	EF
Corporate Governance Report	x		x		x		x			x	x	x	x		x				x	x	x		x	
Recent instruments or standards																								
Integrated Reporting (<IR>)				x							x	x	x	x	x		x	x	x	x	x	x	x	x
Task Force on Climate-Related Financial Disclosures (TCFD)																						x	x	
United Nations Sustainable Development Goals (UNSDGs)																						x		x
Legislative Decree 254																							x	x
Other underlying standards																								
SA8000® Standard						x		x		x		x		x		x		x		x		x		x
ISO 14001—Environmental management				x		x		x		x		x				x		x		x		x		x
ISO 50001—Energy management												x				x		x		x		x		
ISO 9001—Quality assurance		x						x				x												

Legend AR—Annual Report; SR—Sustainability Report; EF—Eni for; IR—Annual Integrated Report social, economic, and environmental characteristics of the energy industry in which Eni operates were first identified internally to determine the key aspects of corporate performance relevant to sustainability. As the then CEO, Paolo Scaroni, outlined:

> *This first Sustainability Report is the result of our overriding commitment to sustainable development. More than just a new approach in reporting to our stakeholders, the Report is part of more wide-ranging initiatives undertaken over the last year and aimed at identifying and taking concrete action. Our goal is to strive for excellence in the overall management of this leading integrated energy company, and build a better future for us all. (Eni Sustainability Report* 2006, *p. 5)*

2007 was a year of successes in Eni's sustainability efforts. The company joined the World Business Council for Sustainable Development (WBCSD), entered into a partnership with MIT for renewable energy, and was admitted to the Dow Jones Sustainability World Index and the FTSE4Good Index. Additionally, it was included in the Climate Disclosure Leadership Index (CDLI), which testifies to its leadership position in the fight against climate change. Further, it improved its ranking from the third quarter to the second quarter of the GS SUSTAIN Focus List of Goldman Sachs[3] and moved from 28th place to 3rd place in Fortune's annual list of the 100 most sustainable companies.

In 2008, Eni announced that its sustainability management model had become fully operational. By this, Eni meant its sustainability planning, monitoring, and control processes had been fully integrated into the company's management system in line with its "integrated thinking management approach". Priority intervention areas, objectives, and action plans had been identified within these areas, and they had been incorporated into a sustainability section of Eni's Strategic Plan for the period 2009–2012, which set the objectives aimed at contributing, either directly or indirectly, to the achievement of the SDGs.

This same year, a new Eni Code of Ethics came into force to replace the previous 1998 Code of Conduct. Workers' rights, the freedom to join a trade union, as well as the "fight against all forms of discrimination, forced and child labour" were explicitly mentioned in the Code. There have been several updates since, in 2014 and, most recently, in 2017. In its current version, the Code places the pursuit of sustainable development objectives at its forefront:

> *In conducting both its activities as an international company and those with its partners, Eni stands up for the protection and promotion of human rights, inalienable and fundamental prerogatives of human beings and basis for the establishment of societies founded on principles of equality, solidarity, repudiation of war, and for the protection of civil and political rights, of social, economic and cultural rights and the so-called third generation rights (self-determination right, right to peace, right to development and protection of the environment). Any form of discrimination, corruption, forced or child labour is rejected. Particular attention is paid to the acknowledgement and safeguarding of the dignity, freedom and equality of human beings, to protection of labour and of the freedom of trade union association, of health, safety, the environment and biodiversity, as well as the set of values*

[3]Introduced in 2007 by Goldman Sachs, the GS SUSTAIN focus list assesses long-term industry leaders in terms of sustainable competitive advantage and effective management of environmental, social and governance risks.

and principles concerning transparency, energy efficiency and sustainable development, in accordance with International Institutions and Conventions. (Eni Code of Ethics 2017a, *p. 4)*

5.2 The <IR> Journey at Eni

Given the strategic industry within which Eni operates, sustainability is a crucial element in maintaining its legitimacy. Eni states that being sustainable means creating value for stakeholders and using resources in such a way as to avoid jeopardising the needs of future generations. In particular, "Eni's mission sets out the company's values regarding climate change, the environment, access to energy, cooperation and partnerships for development, and the respect for people and human rights" (www.eni.com). In line with this statement, Eni's corporate reporting system has been systematically evolving for years. Arguably, what it is now is the result of a long-established corporate culture, which envisages sustainability as one of the drivers for the pursuit of the company's strategic goals. This view of sustainability can be seen as a natural by-product of the strategic industry within which Eni operates; indeed, the level of sustainable development of a company in the energy industry can significantly affect the company's ability to create value (e.g., because of issues related to the corporate image). Possibly for this reason, sustainability has always been genuinely prioritised by Eni's management as a highly important issue.

In 2010, Eni established the Integrated Risk Management System in an attempt to reach a comprehensive and selective view of the business operational risks. In the same year, having published its fourth annual sustainability report, Eni decided to embark on a journey towards <IR>—a coherent decision that reflects the company's intention to integrate sustainability into the company's management system and the firm's overall processes. In 2011, Eni prepared its reports following the principles set out in the IIRC's Pilot Program and launched the new *Eni For* banner to house its sustainability reports, as explained below:

To complete the Integrated Report, Eni For is the new annual sustainability reporting document, which responds to the requirements of our principal stakeholders and, in particular, to the Global Compact. This document clearly and transparently sets out our commitment to the 10 Principles of the Global Compact in corporate action and strategy, as well as our contribution to the development objectives of the United Nations. (Eni For 2011, *p. 88)*

By 2013, Eni was preparing its annual reports in accordance with the <IR> Framework (IIRC 2013) and, in 2014, Eni renamed its annual report to "Integrated Annual Report", which it used up until 2017.

Eni's reporting system relies upon a multi-channel structure which caters for different levels of detail, thus providing a means to effectively address the information needs of its wide range of stakeholders. Additionally, to avoid potential information redundancies while providing comprehensive disclosure, Eni has made use of new technologies. All of its business reports can be downloaded directly from the company's website as a quick and easy avenue to the company's sustainability information. Also, an interactive charting tool makes it easy and convenient for users to analyse Eni's performance by business segment and thematic areas. What clearly emerges from Eni's website is that the company makes genuine attempts to effectively reach multiple audiences. Therefore, Eni appears to demonstrate a long-term commitment to sustainability through its sustainability reports and <IR> as part of its ongoing corporate reporting journey.

Eni's 2017 Integrated Annual Report (2017d, p. 6) "is aimed at representing financial and sustainability performance, underlining the existing connections between competitive environment, group strategy, business model, integrated risk management and a stringent corporate governance system". The report outlines the company's strategy that focuses on creating long-term value for both the company and its stakeholders (see Fig. 5.1).

To pursue its operating objectives, Eni has adopted an integrated strategy that combines financial robustness with environmental and social sustainability. Specifically, Eni's mission is built around three levers: (i) a path to decarbonisation; (ii) an operating model that seeks to reduce the risks associated with the business activity as well as environmental and social impacts; and (iii) a host country cooperation model grounded in long-lasting partnerships. In particular, the 2017 *Eni For* report details

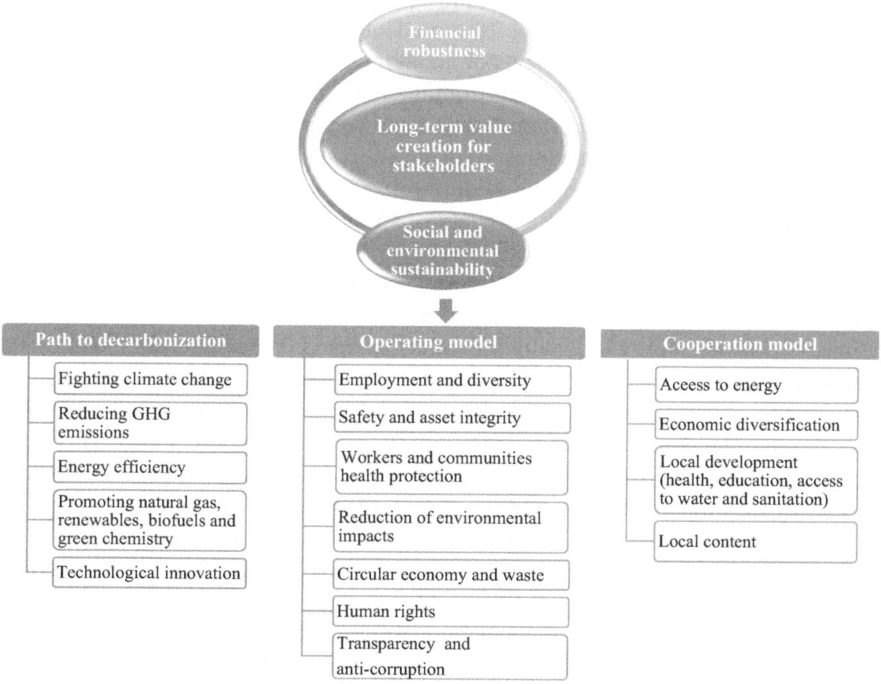

Fig. 5.1 Eni's integrated strategy. *Source* Adapted from 'Eni For' (2017b)

the work undertaken in the area of climate change, its operating model, and its cooperation with communities and third parties (*Eni For* 2017b, p. 7). This reinforces the argument that Eni is a company that takes sustainability-related issues seriously as reflected in its business model.

5.3 <IR> as a Result of an Integrated Thinking Process

Data and information about Eni were mainly collected through semi-structured interviews with three managers in charge of sustainability over the period between November 2013 and April 2015. The timing of the interviews arguably represents a limitation of the case study. According to Qu and Dumay (2011), semi-structured interviews are an appropriate method of data collection for research scenarios like the one in this study, since interviewees can express their thoughts freely, thus revealing hidden aspects of human and organisational behaviour and researchers can follow-up with additional questions if desired. With the permission of the interviewees, each interview was tape-recorded and fully transcribed for the subsequent process of analysis. A total of 13 interviews totalling 10 hours were transcribed, with each interview varying in length from 30 min to two hours and averaging 50 min each. Field notes and informal conversations complemented the taped interviews. As Yin outlines (2014), using "multiple sources of evidence" during data collection helps develop construct validity for a case study. For reasons of anonymity, the three managers are referred to as M1, M2, and M3 when quoting from the interviews.

At Eni, the ideals behind the production of integrated reports appear to be supported by integrated thinking by the company's top management around sustainability. As one of the managers outlined during the interview, "the preparation of the integrated report is the result of a process of strategic integrated thinking, showing the relationship between elements of the scenery and competitive context and Eni's strategic direction and sustainable performance" (M1). According to another manager, "the <IR> drafting process is a way of shedding light on the company's efforts to integrate sustainability gradually into all its business processes" (M2). At Eni, the managers argue that the integrated report is as a document aimed at "illustrating how sustainability constitutes one of the drivers for the pursuit of the company's objectives through the description of results, actions, and future plans" (M3). Therefore, what clearly emerged from the interviews is that the integrated report was certainly viewed by the three managers as being part of a managerial process (i.e., integrated thinking), and not just a communication tool for external stakeholders.

These statements are in line with the IIRC's view that the "cycle of integrated thinking and reporting" will result "in efficient and productive capital allocation" and thereby "act as a force for financial stability and sustainability" (IIRC 2013, p. 2). The idea behind this assumption is that integrated thinking is a breakaway from the traditional 'silo approach' that leads to an organisational strategy with embedded sustainability across the value chain and the necessary and corresponding management control systems. In this regard, Eccles and Krzus (2014, p. 49) point out that emphasis on integrated thinking remains one of the "most important contributions to the meaning of integrated reporting". Whether or not this is true, it does seem clear that the purpose of integrated thinking is to address some of the criticisms of current reporting, such as its inability to create connectivity or to accurately reflect organisational behaviours or information sets (La Torre et al. 2019). As the IIRC itself outlines, integrated thinking is the basis of <IR>, and the two concepts mutually reinforce each other (IIRC 2013, p. 1).

The interviewees, however, acknowledged that the production of an integrated report was not without its challenges. An important aspect that emerged from the interviews is that a significant problem for Eni was how to quantify the contribution of sustainability to the economic result of the company. This was partly attributed to the fact that the <IR> Framework contains little detailed information as to content and does not require the disclosure of either specific key performance indicators or measurement methods. Given the recent IIRC's decision to avoid wholesale changes to the <IR> Framework in favour of minor corrections and clarifications, it is highly likely that Eni's management is and will continue to face such issues in the future.

As discussed earlier, the top management of Eni supports the ideals and production of an integrated report. In turn, this provides support for the view that integrated thinking begins at the upper level of an organisation and guides its *modus operandi*. If this is not the case, it is unlikely that integrated thinking will become a permanent part of an organisation's DNA nor extend through its entire value chain (SAICA 2015). As Massingham et al. (2019) point out, for integrated thinking to work, there must be an integration of corporate culture and corporate governance, both of which cascade down from top management. Eni's apparent success with <IR>, and its explicit connections to integrated thinking, can be contrasted with speculations about the culture and governance of Omega's holding company. At the very least, Omega appears to be a long way behind Eni in its environmental and social performance management processes.

When it comes to the perceived motivation behind <IR>, all the interviewed managers stated that "Socially Responsible Investors (SRIs) have expressed their enthusiasm for the company's efforts to prepare an integrated report". Indeed, in 2011, following the release of the first of Eni's integrated report, the company asked SRIs and traditional financial analysts to provide feedback on the initiative undertaken by the company. Overall, Eni's attempts to provide an integrated depiction of its sustainability business model, and showing how it supports the company's strategy, received positive feedback from SRIs. In contrast, the interviewed managers found that traditional financial analysts had no particular interest in this type of disclosure. Accordingly, the three managers shared the view that Eni's adoption of <IR> was considered useful for a small group of SRIs rather than all providers of financial capital. This starkly contrasts with the IIRC's claim that <IR> will be of interest more generally within stock markets.

It should be borne in mind that, at Eni, integrated reports have not replaced sustainability reports. Rather, one supplements the other. While this typically leads to a certain level of redundancy in the information conveyed to the market, it does not, however, result in reduced clarity for investors engaged in socially responsible investing or, more generally, for stakeholders. Eni has taken particular care to provide mechanisms that allow stakeholders to select the information they deem relevant directly from the company's website. This reinforces the argument that Eni's strategies and solutions for communicating with stakeholders are genuine.

5.3.1 Other Reporting Frameworks

Eni's commitment to environmental and social performance is also demonstrated in its commitment to reporting on the UNSDGs. As outlined in the 2017 *Eni For* report (2017b), the UNSDGs are connected to specific initiatives in the company.

> *As part of the Columbia Center on Sustainable Investment's analysis, Eni's initiatives, governance systems and incentive mechanisms were reviewed. The report found that Eni has initiatives impacting all 17 SDGs. The company is particularly committed to contributing to the achievement of SDGs 7 (affordable and clean energy) and 8 (decent work and economic growth). Its health and education programs for employees and communities contribute to SDGs 3 (good health and well-being) and 4 (quality education) in many Countries of operation. Significant efforts have been placed to follow best practices regarding environmental monitoring and reporting to avoid negative impacts on SDGs 14 (life below water) and 15 (life on land). In the last few years, a number of climate change activities have been developed that help address SDG 13 (climate action). The report recognizes these important steps and encourages additional plans and timelines in respect of the objectives of the Paris Climate Agreement. The report also emphasizes further opportunities to bolster SDGs 5 and 10 through gender-sensitive and participatory processes in local interventions. Furthermore, in line with SDG 17, Eni is committed to sharing competencies and economic resources with a variety of organizations toward the achievement of the SDGs. (Eni For* 2017b, *p. 12)*

Additionally, Eni has been a member of the TCFD since it was established. This involvement is featured in the 2016 *Eni For* report's risk management framework:

> *The process for managing the risks and opportunities associated with climate change is carried out by considering 5 drivers, in line with the recommendations of the Task Force on Climate Related Financial Disclosure, of which Eni is a member. Climate change risk identifies the possibility of changes occurring to aspects associated with climate change which may generate, in the short, medium and long term, physical and other risks which impact on the business. (Eni For* 2016, *p. 13)*

In its 2017 Integrated Annual Report, Eni boasts about being the only company in the oil and gas industry to take part in the Financial Stability Board's TCFD. In June 2017, the TCFD published voluntary recommendations to encourage effective disclosures on the financial implications of climate change. In response, Eni prepared a special report on its path to decarbonisation that illustrates how it is addressing the crucial challenge of the energy industry and how it plans to meet the recommendations laid down by the TCFD. The *Eni For 2017—Path to Decarbonisation* (2017c, p. 7) states:

> *Eni has undertaken a decarbonization path to meet the crucial challenge of the energy industry: the transition to a low carbon future and the access to resources for a growing*

world population. In this direction, the strategy adopted includes, in addition to the reduction of direct GHG emissions, a resilient portfolio of hydrocarbons in which natural gas plays a central role, the development of green businesses and the commitment to the research and development of innovative solutions to support all the activities.

Eni commits itself to a 'gradual implementation' of those recommendations, identifying four affected areas of its business[4]:

- **Governance**: Disclose the organisation's governance around climate-related risks and opportunities.
- **Strategy**: Disclose the actual and potential impacts of climate-related risks and opportunities on the organisation's businesses, strategy, and financial planning where such information is material.
- **Risk Management**: Disclose how the organisation identifies, assesses, and manages climate-related risks.
- **Metrics and Targets**: Disclose the metrics and targets used to assess and manage relevant climate-related risks and opportunities where such information is material.

Additionally, Eni does not shy away from bad news. As plainly stated in Eni's 2017 Integrated Annual Report, the group feels that growing worldwide public concerns over GHGs, climate change, and the threat of additional regulations will have adverse effects in the short, medium, and long-term that will result in increased operating costs, reduced profits, and lower shareholder returns:

Rising public concern related to climate change has led and could lead to the adoption of worldwide laws and regulations which could result in a decrease of demand for hydrocarbons and increased compliance costs for the Company. Eni is also exposed to risks of technological breakthrough in the energy field and risks of extreme meteorological events linked to the climate change. All these developments may adversely affect the Group's profitability, businesses outlook and reputation. (Eni Integrated Annual Report 2017d, *p. 85)*

5.3.2 *Other Underlying Standards*

As mentioned earlier, Eni also complies with several different international and industry standards, such as ISO 14001, ISO 50001, ISO 9001 and SA8000® Standard, that serve as evidence that the company complies with social initiatives in environment, energy, quality assurance and socially responsible employment practices. Taken at face value, Eni appears to be genuinely interested in its environmental and social commitment and has consistently taken steps to improve its performance. Eni 'walks the talk' by developing strategies and solutions to issues of worth over value and by communicating its goals and progress with all stakeholders, not just its stock market participants. In conclusion, the evidence from the case provides strong support for the argument that Eni's journey towards <IR> has been independent, entirely voluntary, and the result of an internal call to foster sustainability. There has been

[4]Eni 2017 Integrated Annual Report (2017d, p. 94).

a genuine effort to improve reporting practices from a company whose culture has always valued reporting as a primary means of external corporate communication. These insights, and those from the Leonardo case, are compared and discussed in more detail in the next chapter.

References

Eccles, R. G., & Krzus, M. P. (2014). *The integrated reporting movement: Meaning, momentum, motives, and materiality*. Wiley.

Eni. (2006). *Eni sustainability report.*

Eni. (2011). *Eni For 2011.* Available at: https://www.eni.com/en_IT/documentations.page?categoryCode=sustainability. Accessed September 12, 2019.

Eni (2016). *Eni For 2016.* Available at: https://www.eni.com/en_IT/documentations.page?categoryCode=sustainability Accessed September 21, 2019.

Eni. (2017a). *Eni code of ethics.* Available at: https://www.eni.com/en_IT/results.page?question=eni+code+of+ethics. Accessed September 25, 2019.

Eni. (2017b). *Eni For 2017.* Available at: https://www.eni.com/en_IT/documentations.page?categoryCode=sustainability. Accessed September 27, 2019.

Eni. (2017c). *Eni For 2017—Decarbonization.* Available at: https://www.eni.com/en_IT/documentations.page?categoryCode=sustainability. Accessed September 25, 2019.

Eni. (2017d). *Eni integrated annual report.* Available at: https://www.eni.com/en_IT/documentations.page. Accessed October 3, 2019.

Eni. (2018). *Eni annual report.* Available at: https://www.eni.com/en_IT/documentations.page. Accessed October 12, 2019.

International Integrated Reporting Council (IIRC). (2013). *The international <IR> framework.* London: International Integrated Reporting Council. Available at: http://www.integratedreporting.org/wp-content/uploads/2015/03/13-12-08-THE-INTERNATIONAL-IR-FRAMEWORK-2-1.pdf. Accessed October 1, 2019.

La Torre, M., Bernardi, C., Guthrie, J., & Dumay, J. (2019). Integrated reporting and integrated thinking: Practical challenges. In S. Arvidsson (Ed.), *Challenges in managing sustainable business* (pp. 25–54). Cham: Palgrave Macmillan. https://doi.org/10.1007/978-3-319-93266-8_2.

Massingham, R., Massingham, P. R., & Dumay, J. (2019). Improving integrated reporting: A new learning and growth perspective for the balanced scorecard. *Journal of Intellectual Capital, 20*(1), 60–82. https://doi.org/10.1108/JIC-06-2018-0095.

Qu, S. Q., & Dumay, J. (2011). The qualitative research interview. *Qualitative Research in Accounting & Management, 8*(3), 238–264. https://doi.org/10.1108/11766091111162070.

South African Institute of Chartered Accountants (SAICA). (2015). *Integrated thinking—An exploratory survey.* Available at: http://integratedreportingsa.org/ircsa/wp-content/uploads/2017/05/SAICAIntegratedThinkingLandscape.pdf. Accessed November 4, 2019.

Yin, R. K. (2014). *Case study research. Design and methods.* Thousand Oaks, California: Sage.

Chapter 6
<IR>: Foray or Mainstay?

Abstract The two cases presented in this book are diametrically opposed, and each raises different insights for <IR> practice. However, both offer some lessons for furthering the <IR> Framework. They also offer scope to learn some lessons about corporate disclosure. These lessons outline how <IR> works differently in practice. Thus, these two cases help to conceptualise how companies treat <IR>, and what they hope to achieve by implementing it (or not). Such lessons are needed because we cannot always accept unquestioningly that new management technologies will or should be adopted. Nor can we be sure that managers will accept the claims espoused by <IR>'s proponents or that its alleged benefits will always be realised.

6.1 Insights from Omega

The first case study illustrates the motivations that led Omega to its journey towards integrated thinking and, eventually, to the adoption of <IR> by its holding company. Management concern over how to survive in the competitive aerospace and defence sector inspired a research project into how to unlock the company's IC. Initially, the goal was to produce a report for use in decision-making. Any change made to support new decision-making processes is interesting because it signals an awareness by management that a company needs to do something differently.

What is apparent in the Omega case is that the idea of integrating the financial and non-financial information to evaluate organisational performance emerged from the research project as a top-down initiative by its CEO and Omega was one short step from producing its own form of integrated reporting if only its CEO had not resigned. Interestingly, however, the project's original goal of managerial decision support sits in stark contrast to <IR>'s primary purpose of disclosing information to the providers of financial capital (IIRC 2013). Additionally, to truly succeed, <IR> requires integrated thinking. A 'tone at the top' form of management control can propel integrated thinking throughout a company. Nonetheless, the risk with this form of impetus is that usually the initiative only survives as long as the CEO survives (Merchant and Van der Stede 2007). Research into the related field of IC, the predecessor to <IR>, confirms this observation, showing how powerful actors

C. Bernardi, *Implementing Integrated Reporting*, SpringerBriefs in Accounting,
https://doi.org/10.1007/978-3-030-11193-9_6

like CEOs reinforce their "social capital and [their] right to develop IC practices", while at the same time linking their authority to the potential power of <IR> (Dumay and Rooney 2018, p. 256). After all, it is the CEO's job to lead the organisation, and such an important change to management practice requires not just the sanction but also the support of the company's most powerful actors.

However, changes to management are inevitable in companies, and sometimes the role of CEOs is short-lived. For example, the average tenure of a CEO in Italy is about five years (Ennser-Jedenastik 2014). So, this poses a problem for <IR>, and other popular management systems, such as IC or the Balanced Scorecard, if different managers resort to different management systems to promote their agendas. As demonstrated in the Omega case, the broom of management change swept integrated reporting away alongside its CEO champion, and the next regime ushered in a commitment to sustainability, a listing on the DJSI, and a suite of reporting technologies more suited to those performance indicators. The Omega case vividly depicts how integrated reporting was doomed without continued support from top management. More tellingly, given that <IR> is not a bottom-up initiative, one can, therefore, argue that it is similarly vulnerable in any other company.

Vestiges of integrated reporting have, however, resurfaced in Omega's current incarnation as a division of Leonardo—not because of integrated thinking in the group overall or because <IR> is a revolution in corporate reporting, but because it can be used to comply with some aspects of the new EU Directive (2014). While Leonardo's journey towards < IR> is evolving according to the operational environmental challenges it faces, it is still unclear what else the management seeks to achieve by (re)introducing <IR>. Potentially, it could be an exercise to convey a positive impression to stakeholders, which would influence Leonardo's choice of reporting framework. As Dumay et al. (2017) outline, using <IR> allows flexibility for a company to respond to the changing operational and legislative environment. Therefore, it could be that adopting <IR> is a "structurally determined" mechanism to "strategically respond" to the pressures of stakeholders. In the end, however, it is hard to avoid noticing the chasm between a motivation to respond to external forces and the need to communicate more effectively with financial capital providers.

6.2 Insights from Eni

The second case study explores how <IR> evolved into established practice within Eni from its very beginnings. Eni's current reporting system, which now includes <IR>, is the result of a journey in the making and the product of a corporate culture that has always pursued sustainability as a priority goal. Perhaps Eni's view of sustainability reporting is a natural by-product of its operations in the fossil fuel energy sector, where a company's image of handling environmental issues can significantly affect its ability to create value. Yet, Eni's motivations seem to be deeper and more sincere. Its culture is based on the business philosophy of its founder, Enrico Mattei, and extends to creating positive impacts for its employees' well-being and onward through society. For this reason, sustainability has always been genuinely prioritised by Eni's management as a highly important issue.

When Eni's independent and entirely voluntary journey towards <IR> began in 2010, it had already been producing sustainability reports and disclosing other non-financial information for four years. Its first official 'integrated report' followed in 2011. Therefore, for Eni, <IR> was the result of an internal calling and the summation of initiatives undertaken in previous years to foster sustainability. The arrival of <IR> as a reporting technology, and an easily-acceptable ideology, blended well with an already progressive corporate culture that valued reporting as a primary means of external corporate communication. It appears that adopting <IR> was a spontaneous and rationally sound attempt to improve its organisational reporting practices, by gathering and implementing new concepts, models, and guidelines (see Lounsboury 2008).

Notably, Eni's integrated report is not a replacement for its sustainability report. Rather, the two complement each other. The company's commitment to producing multiple reports suggests several things. First, it uses different communication channels to target specific audiences to develop and support its legitimacy (Suchman 1995; Dumay et al. 2015). Second, Eni apparently perceives a clear separation between the principles of <IR> and its other forms of reporting, such as the GRI. Third, Eni seems to see the GRI as a better choice to the <IR> Framework for communicating social and environmental sustainability, which is interesting since this was <IR>'s original goal.

6.3 Linking the Cases to Contemporary Issues for <IR>

The IIRC claims that today's fast-moving markets and international trends encourage the adoption of <IR> (IIRC 2014, p. 3). Although <IR> presents significant potential challenges and opportunities, considerable scepticism persists as to whether <IR> is the right answer for the argued deficiencies of financial reporting. Further, like all novel initiatives in the corporate reporting field, <IR> is the object of worldwide international debate among both academics and practitioners as regards to its implementation (Dumay et al. 2017). Against this background, some organisations are experimenting with <IR> according to the IIRC's <IR> database and corporateregister.com,[1] but many others come and go. However, in most jurisdictions, such as the US, there is less uptake of <IR> than the IIRC would desire.

[1] http://www.corporateregister.com/frameworks/iirc/. Accessed November 3, 2019.

6.3.1 Is <IR> Running Out of Steam?

While <IR> seems to have gained some traction, it may have begun to stall. For example, some organisations who were part of the initial foray into <IR> no longer produce integrated reports, such as Bank Australia (formerly Bank Mecu). Beyond the product uptake implications, this is also a financial concern for <IR> because the companies that were part of the <IR> Pilot Programme paid a significant fee for the privilege of participating in support of the IIRC. In 2012, the Pilot Programme contributions were £846,563. The 2017 equivalent, "<IR> Network" contributions, fell to only £559,273, which shows how much financial and, most likely, moral support has eroded since the IIRC's inception. Even contributions from Council members have fallen—down from £724,320 in 2016 to £663,205 in 2017—demonstrating deterioration in the IIRC's very foundations. In 2018, the trend reversed slightly, with "<IR> Network" contributions rising to approximately £564,000 and Council member contributions of approximately £711,000.

The possibility of financial peril for the IIRC was a very real possibility in 2017. If it had not been for the injection of £304,842 by way of a £200,000 grant from a registered charity called The Integrated Reporting Foundation along with funds from some other undisclosed sources, the IIRC would have incurred a significant financial deficit in addition to the £21,930 shortfall reported in its 2017 financial statements. Subtract around £300 k from its £581,464 retained surplus and more than half its worth would have been wiped out. Similarly, in 2018 the IIRC received more than £497 k in grants from the Integrated Reporting Foundation, most of which has ended up as a liability as accruals and deferred income is now more than £1 m. However, the grants to the Integrated Reporting Foundation were funded by another charity called the Fortune Trust, who had a balance of just over £481 k as at April 2017. No accounts have been issued by the Fortune Trust since then, and if that is the main source of the IIRC's £497 k in grant money, that source may have already dried up for 2019. Even the IIRC recognises its council/network funding model is approaching its use-by date. Therefore, without either significantly increasing income or trimming expenses, the IIRC will continue to burn cash as it has consistently done since 2014, and poor cash flow will threaten its ability to promote <IR>.

The IIRC's own integrated report (2017, p. 35) discloses the following challenges to expanding its revenue sources:

- The IIRC has a relatively complex 'sell' compared to more traditional causes which address singular issues.
- There is a need for greater urgency in its vision, and defined timelines to get funders' attention.
- Funders are increasingly moving away from 'unrestricted funding'—the IIRC needs to 'package' its work into discrete fundable pieces of work.
- The IIRC's fundraising space is very crowded with a limited pool of funders.
- Funders do not want to see duplication of effort, but much greater collaboration between organisations.

So concerned was the IIRC about the drop in its core income that a full-time team member dedicated to fundraising was appointed in January 2018. Also, the IIRC received a further grant of £323,000 in 2018 from The Integrated Reporting Foundation, registering a total comprehensive income of £66,000 for that year.

6.3.2 Lack of the Take-up Claimed by the IIRC

Another key problem is the lack of take-up of <IR>. While the IIRC claims that more than 1600 companies across 64 countries are now preparing integrated reports, there is scant evidence to support this claim. It has been eight years since the IIRC formed, and yet when we look at the jurisdictions that are the targets of <IR>, it is hard to find evidence that <IR> is becoming the corporate reporting norm. Three key regions, however, stand out as examples: the UK, South Africa, and Japan.

The UK is the IIRC's home base and is a prime example of how <IR> has failed to get the support it desperately needs to remain viable. According to the corporateregister.com website,[2] only 78 <IR> reports by 33 different organisations were issued in the five years from 2013 to 2017 across the UK. Moreover, production is decreasing not increasing, with 13 reports produced in 2017 compared to 17 in 2016. Relative to the 748 CSR and sustainability reports published in the UK in 2017, <IR> accounts for just a mere fraction (1.7%). These numbers show <IR> is far from the corporate reporting norm.

In South Africa, <IR> is advocated as a good framework for complying with the King IV corporate governance guidelines (IoDSA 2016). But, according to corporateregister.com, in 2017, <IR> was still used less than other forms of CSR and sustainability reporting by a count of 194–302 reports. However, the pressure on South African companies to follow <IR> does appear to have significantly lowered the use of the GRI. While seemingly a boon for the IIRC, this increase in 'market share' raises some moral questions. Arguably, there can only be adverse effects from reducing GRI reporting in a country that is so rich in natural resources and where social and environmental sustainability concerns should be paramount. <IR> is not so much concerned with the business case for sustainability as it is concerned for the sustainability of business (Flower 2015; Thomson 2015). Given the investor-driven basis for sustainability in <IR> (Howitt and Thurm 2018), it appears that rampant capitalism is once again triumphing over society and the environment (La Torre et al. 2019).

In Italy, where the two case studies are based, support for <IR> is somewhat more popular, but take-up is still extremely low—i.e., in 2017, corporateregister.com identified 352 reports of which only 25 (7.1%) were classified as integrated reports. In the two cases presented, each company turned to <IR> for different reasons but neither was seeking <IR>'s primary benefit of "financial stability and sustainability"

[2] http://www.corporateregister.com/frameworks/iirc/region/?r=UK. Accessed November 9, 2019.

as a primary goal. So then why did these companies undertake <IR> in the first place? Understanding this may be key to our understanding of the <IR> phenomenon.

Another development, as evidenced in the Eni case, is that many organisations claim to publish an integrated report but also use different frameworks such as the GRI to complement or supplement <IR>'s lack of engagement with social and environmental concerns (Milne and Gray 2013; Flower 2015). The Eni case in particular shows that <IR> is an incomplete paradigm in the cluttered world of corporate reporting. The analysis and corporate reporting tables presented in the previous chapters are ample evidence of how <IR > has become one cobblestone among many paving the corporate reporting road, rather than a centre line guiding the journey ahead.

Further evidence to support the multi-framework approach to reporting is found in Japan, where the Mitsubishi Corporation, a leading proponent of <IR >, has been issuing an integrated report since 2014. In its latest 2017 integrated report, Mitsubishi combined the <IR> Framework, the GRI, ISO 2600, and the UNSDGs. From an integrated report to an "integration of reporting" (Monciardini et al. 2016), this does not bode well for the IIRC. The criticism levelled at <IR> for not being comprehensive and inclusive of social and environmental sustainability concerns seems well-founded given the ample evidence to show that when <IR> is applied in practice, companies need to make up for its deficiencies by marrying it with other reporting frameworks. Therefore, I argue that the incompleteness of < IR> demands an urgent debate between practitioners, policymakers, and thought leaders from around the world about harmonising the plethora of reporting frameworks and standards.

There is cause to believe that the IIRC is not only cognizant of < IR>'s deficiencies but also the deficiencies of other frameworks. In its own attempt at harmonisation, it has established the "The Better Alignment Project", driven by a group called the Corporate Reporting Dialogue, with the aim of harmonising the different reporting frameworks to "make it easier for companies to prepare effective and coherent disclosures that meet the information needs of capital markets and society" (see, https://corporatereportingdialogue.com/better-alignment-project/#alignment). As outlined on the IIRC's website.[3]

> Participants of the Corporate Reporting Dialogue have committed to driving better alignment of sustainability reporting frameworks, as well as with frameworks that promote further integration between non-financial and financial reporting.

The Corporate Reporting Dialogue is a virtual who's who of social and environmental sustainability groups, each advocating their own brand of reporting. Members include the Climate Disclosure Standards Board (CDSB), the Climate Disclosure Project (CDP), the GRI, the Sustainability Accounting Standards Board (SASB), and of course, the IIRC. The project is ambitious, but it is hard to see how a harmonious consensus can be reached given the IIRC's goal to become the corporate reporting norm.

Further, without wishing to be pessimistic, past experience at similar endeavours should have taught us some lessons. The failure to reconcile US GAAP with IFRS

[3] http://integratedreporting.org/corporate-reporting-dialogue/. Accessed October 21, 2019.

after decades of talk, albeit with some progress, suggests it is unlikely we will see a harmonised non-financial reporting framework emerge from a co-operative laden with individual agendas initiated by an organisation that must act foremost in the interests of its financial backers. As long as the IIRC continues to advocate <IR> as the next corporate reporting norm without including the business of sustainability as one of its central tenets, I fail to see how the other framework proponents would agree to the IIRC's claim to rightfully dominate the corporate reporting landscape.

6.4 <IR> Practice and not Rhetoric Is Needed to Understand Its Utility

At the time of writing this book, <IR> was clearly a hot topic among academic researchers. Initially, the majority of scholars were supportive of <IR> as a new reporting mechanism and hopeful that it would deal with the alleged deficiencies of financial reporting (de Villiers et al. 2014). The result was an explosion of academic research into <IR> and its impacts. So much so that one colleague laments, "there are now more academic articles written about <IR> than there are actual integrated reports" and "there are more universities studying <IR> than there are companies issuing integrated reports". However, the fact that so many researchers are concerned with <IR> shows that the <IR> movement is not trivial and warrants rigorous research (Dumay et al. 2016).

What distinctly emerges from Chap. 3 is that most of the academic literature adopts a top-down perspective, which is characteristic of first- and second-stage research (Guthrie et al. 2012). First-stage research focuses on raising awareness of a specific research field's potential (Petty and Guthrie 2000, p. 155), while second-stage research deals with understanding the ostensive impact of <IR>. Third-stage research, however, focuses on the performative not the normative aspect (Dumay et al. 2016). Hence, much more third-stage research would be expected should <IR> become the corporate reporting norm. Performative, empirical studies help to develop understandings of how to apply <IR> in practice and whether the normative prescriptions espoused by the IIRC either work or do not work—generally and/or in specific contexts. Since <IR> is a relatively recent phenomenon, it will probably take quite a long time before it is possible to ascertain its potential costs and benefits and, more importantly, whether <IR> is useful to organisations.

The Eni case raises a number of issues. Eni's managers believe that SRIs use their integrated reports which, if true, raises questions about *how* those analysts are using the reports. Conceivably, fund managers with an socially responsible 'style' must make two relevant determinations: Is the company suitable for inclusion in an SRI fund? Is the integrated report helpful in deciding Eni's proportion of a portfolio? Hence, it is important to understand the role of an integrated report in such screening processes both in isolation and in conjunction with other information. However, it is worth emphasising that Eni's beliefs are not proven. It may just be that Eni's management believes and promotes the rhetoric surrounding <IR>. It could also be that very human tendency to conceptualise benefits as justifications of one's decisions.

If the answers are that the integrated report is only being used for screening, but not for financial decision-making, it would suggest that the informational value for investors is not as high as argued by the IIRC. If the answer is that the information is used for financial decision-making, this raises the issue of why non-SRI analysts interviewed by Eni did not find it relevant, and why there might be a contrast between SRI analysts and purely financial analysts. The case of Eni also raises the issue of whether and how integrated reports and sustainability reports are used as distinct documents by analysts.

Reflections on the value of < IR> to analysts are controversial. A study by Abhayawansa et al. (2016) finds that most analysts covering companies in the IIRC Pilot Programme barely knew what <IR> was, let alone found <IR> useful for their work. Dumay (2016, p. 178) supports the view that it is not possible for integrated reports (and even IC reports) to contain significant amounts of information to better inform investors about a listed company's prospects:

> The value to investors for all forms of reports beyond regulated financial reports is questionable. Imagine if an investment advisor waited for the latest integrated or IC report before making a recommendation to buy or sell shares. I suspect the advisor would soon be searching for another job because the timeliness and value of these reports are not relevant to active investors.

However, there are a number of studies that have investigated the benefits from a financial market perspective associated with the mandated integrated reporting in the South African context (where the International <IR> Framework has been endorsed as good practice on how to prepare an integrated report). Perhaps the most telling study is by Atkins and Maroun (2015), who illustrate that South African investors still advocate for integrated reporting despite its obstacles and their own concerns. In their paper, Lee and Yeo (2016) demonstrate a positive correlation between a company's compliance with integrated reporting and its market value, especially for firms with highly complex organisational structures or with a greater need for outside financing. Zhou et al. (2017) study shows that the more a company's reports align with the <IR> framework, the fewer errors the forecast analysts make. For some firms, reporting even reduces the cost of equity capital. Bernardi and Stark (2018, p. 16), "provide some support for those who advocate the virtues of integrated reporting". In examining the mandate for integrated reporting in South Africa and the subsequent impact on the accuracy of analyst one year-ahead forecasts of earnings, they find support for their theory that that ESG disclosure levels, in particular environmental ones, are associated with forecast accuracy after the introduction of the integrated reporting regime. Baboukardos and Rimmel (2016) reach a similar conclusion that integrated reporting lends additional relevance to financial statements for investors, which may ultimately lead to value creation. Finally, Barth et al. (2017) analyse whether integrated report quality is associated with firm value. The authors find evidence that integrated reporting quality is significantly associated with a firm's stock liquidity and expected future cash flows.

6.5 Understanding the <IR> Journey into the Future

To conclude our journey into understanding <IR>, I want to reflect on what the future holds for <IR>. Is it just another management fashion fad that will soon pass by? Or is it a management technology that still holds promise? In its current iteration, <IR> portends better communication with investors and more efficient capital allocation. Such claims are relevant because <IR> was born in response to the disaster that was the Global Financial Crisis. It was a way for the accounting profession to regain some of its lost legitimacy (Gleeson-White 2014), and for corporations to counter the public pressure for more transparency (Bartels et al. 2016). In retrospect, it seems clear that the IIRC made a mistake in discarding social and economic sustainability from its framework (Flower 2015; Thomson, 2015). Will this be a fatal mistake? Only time will tell.

In the meantime, the IIRC keeps going. While funding has dwindled, its war chest is still substantial enough to continue promoting its agenda. As long as the IIRC can continue to raise funds to keep its operations afloat, it will march on with its campaign. However, should the income from traditional sources continue to dry up, the future may not look so rosy. The main problem is that not every company that experiments with <IR> stays on the journey. As a result, the IIRC seems, at best, to be stagnating, at worst, losing support. Beyond the financial problems from discontinued <IR> Network support, there are also reputational consequences when companies abandon <IR > in search of more comprehensive frameworks. While the IIRC has openly stated that it wants to remain a voluntary framework, it can never hope to become the corporate reporting norm without significant regulatory support (Flower 2015; Stubbs and Higgins 2018). Simply look at South Africa where corporate law actively endorses the <IR> Framework and still the alternatives are used more.

Another double-edged sword for the IIRC and <IR> is the European Directive (Directive 2014/95/EU). This legislation, coupled with previous CEO Richard Howitt's connections to both the EU Council and the IIRC, provided a great opportunity for the IIRC to find a new purchase as a tool for compliance. However, the threat of competition from rival frameworks, such as the GRI, is already apparent. The GRI has issued guidance on how to comply with the EU Directive (GRI and Global Sustainability Standards Board 2017) and it is already the most used non-financial reporting framework in Europe. The GRI and Global Sustainability Standards Board (2017) guidelines advocate that companies only need minor adjustments to their current GRI reporting to comply with the new legislation, so it is not surprising that Howitt and the IIRC had a tough time convincing companies to switch to <IR>. The Leonardo case shows that <IR> can be used to comply with the EU Directive, but this seems to be the exception, not the rule.

To even come close to being the corporate reporting norm, the IIRC needs to win the hearts and minds of the managers and policymakers of a nation. Take-up cannot be on a company-by-company basis. There must be a groundswell of broad support. So far, the IIRC has mostly concentrated on winning the hearts of regulators.

It claims that regulators, stock exchanges, and professional accounting associations in many countries support the IIRC and <IR> (IIRC 2017). It boasts over some form of "adoption" in "64 countries, including every G20 economy"[4]. But charming the regulators does not equate to engaging the C-suite, which is essential for turning support into voluntary compliance by companies.

One notable exception is Japan, where there is probably a greater level of take-up than elsewhere in the world. As with other jurisdictions, Japan is prone to the "integration of reporting" (Sabelfeld and Dumay 2018). However, it also has a unique social and political environment. It is grappling with changes in corporate governance guidelines, corporate scandals, and a general lack of trust in the transparency of Japanese business practices by foreigners. Competition for funds in the world's capital markets has driven regulators, the accounting profession, and many companies to an answer for these criticisms, and many have thrown their support behind <IR>.

However, Japan is only one major market. The IIRC has turned its attention to other potential jewels for its crown as part of its "Breaking Through" strategy—especially the US and China (IIRC 2017), and beyond with its, perhaps somewhat premature, 'Momentum Phase'. Breaking into these markets will be a challenge since the US has already been a focus for the IIRC but gained little traction. Adams (2018, p. 365) outlines additional obstacles to conquering the US because "public companies are already subject to an extensive and well-established reporting environment", e.g., the 10-K report that covers many of the same issues as <IR>. China will also be particularly difficult to sway considering that many companies are beholden to the Chinese State as their largest shareholder. Thus, Chinese regulators tend to both adopt and adapt international accounting regulations to suit their own social, political, and economic whims (see Baker et al. 2010 for a detailed example). It is therefore reasonable to conclude that the new IIRC strategy is ambitious, if not overly optimistic.

One last item to note is the recent developments at the IIRC to shake its reputation for not being compatible with sustainability reporting. Recently, Adams (2017) published a document for the IIRC that explains how <IR> could be used to report on the UNSDGs. Since then, the IIRC has been openly promoting the <IR> Framework as tool organisations can use to report on UNSDGs activities and outcomes. It has also become involved with other reporting frameworks to develop indicators for reporting on the UNSDGs (UNCTAD 2019). Unlike the GRI, that has specific indicators for complying with its own framework, the indicators developed by the UNCTAD can be used in any report and are not specific to the <IR> Framework exclusively. Only time will tell the direction <IR > journey will take for policymakers, stock exchanges, companies, stakeholders, and the IIRC. However, as shown in the two cases, <IR> is merely one part of an ever-evolving corporate reporting landscape.

---

[4]https://integratedreporting.org/integratedreport2017/index_desktop.html. Accessed October 15, 2019.

References

Abhayawansa, S., Elijido-Ten, E., & Dumay, J. (2016). A practice theoretical analysis of the irrelevance of integrated reporting to mainstream sell-side analysts. *Accounting & Finance, 59*(3), 1615–1647. https://doi.org/10.1111/acfi.12367.

Adams, C. (2017). The sustainable development goals, integrated thinking and the integrated report. Available at: https://integratedreporting.org/resource/sdgs-integrated-thinking-and-the-integrated-report/ (Accessed September 8, 2019).

Adams, M. (2018). Emerging integrated reporting practices in the United States. In J. Guthrie, J. Dumay, F. Ricceri, & C. Nielsen (Eds.), *The routledge companion to intellectual capital: Frontiers of research, practice and knowledge* (pp. 365–379). Routledge: London.

Atkins, J., & Maroun, W. (2015). Integrated reporting in South Africa in 2012: Perspectives from South African institutional investors. *Meditari Accountancy Research, 23*(2), 197–221. https://doi.org/10.1108/MEDAR-07-2014-0047.

Baboukardos, D., & Rimmel, G. (2016). Value relevance of accounting information under an integrated reporting approach: A research note. *Journal of Accounting and Public Policy, 35*(4), 437–452. https://doi.org/10.1016/j.jaccpubpol.2016.04.004.

Baker, C. R., Biondi, Y., & Zhang, Q. (2010). Disharmony in international accounting standards setting: The Chinese approach to accounting for business combinations. *Critical Perspectives on Accounting, 21*(2), 107–117. https://doi.org/10.1016/j.cpa.2009.11.004.

Bartels, W., Fogelberg, T., Hoballah, A., van der Lugt, C. T. (2016). Carrots sticks: Global trends in sustainability reporting regulation and policy, KPMG; Global Reporting Initiative (GRI); United Nations Environment Programme; Centre for Corporate Governance in South Africa, Amsterdam. Available at: https://assets.kpmg/content/dam/kpmg/pdf/2016/05/carrots-and-sticks-may-2016.pdf.

Barth, M. E., Cahan, S. F., Chen, L., & Venter, E. R. (2017). The economic consequences associated with integrated report quality: Capital market and real effects. *Accounting, Organizations and Society, 62*, 43–64. https://doi.org/10.1016/j.aos.2017.08.005.

Bernardi, C., & Stark, A. W. (2018). Environmental, social and governance disclosure, integrated reporting, and the accuracy of analyst forecasts. *The British Accounting Review, 50*(1), 16–31. https://doi.org/10.1016/j.bar.2016.10.001.

de Villiers, C., Rinaldi, L., & Unerman, J. (2014). Integrated Reporting: Insights, gaps and an agenda for future research. *Accounting, Auditing & Accountability Journal, 27*(7), 1042–1067. https://doi.org/10.1108/AAAJ-06-2014-1736.

Dumay, J. (2016). A critical reflection on the future of intellectual capital: From reporting to disclosure. *Journal of Intellectual Capital, 17*(1), 168–184. https://doi.org/10.1108/JIC-08-2015-0072.

Dumay, J., & Rooney, J. (2018). Overcoming the symbolic violence of orthodox accounting practice: An intellectual capital perspective. *Journal of Intellectual Capital, 19*(2), 248–271. https://doi.org/10.1108/JIC-02-2017-0026.

Dumay, J., Frost, G., & Beck, C. (2015). Material legitimacy: Blending organisational and stakeholder concerns through non-financial information disclosures. *Journal of Accounting & Organizational Change, 11*(1), 2–23. https://doi.org/10.1108/JAOC-06-2013-0057.

Dumay, J., Bernardi, C., Guthrie, J., & Demartini, P. (2016). Integrated reporting: A structured literature review. *Accounting Forum, 40*(3), 166–185. https://doi.org/10.1016/j.accfor.2016.06.001.

Dumay, J., Bernardi, C., Guthrie, J., & La Torre, M. (2017). Barriers to implementing the international integrated reporting framework: A contemporary academic perspective. *Meditari Accountancy Research, 25*(4), 461–480. https://doi.org/10.1108/MEDAR-05-2017-0150.

Ennser-Jedenastik, L. (2014). Credibility versus control: Agency independence and partisan influence in the regulatory state. *Comparative Political Studies, 48*(7), 823–853. https://doi.org/10.1177/0010414014558259.

European Union. (2014). *Directive 2014/95/EU of the European Parliament and of the Council*. Available at: https://eur-lex.europa.eu/legal-content/EN/TXT/?uri=CELEX%3A32014L0095.

Flower, J. (2015). The international integrated reporting council: A story of failure. *Critical Perspectives on Accounting, 27*, 1–17. https://doi.org/10.1016/j.cpa.2014.07.002.

Gleeson-White, J. (2014). *Six capitals: The revolution capitalism has to have-or can accountants save the planet?*. Sydney: Allen & Unwin.

Global Reporting Initiative (GRI) and Global Sustainability Standards Board. (2017). Linking the GRI standards and the European directive on non-financial and diversity disclosure. Available at: https://www.globalreporting.org/standards/resource-download-center/linking-gri-standards-and-european-directive-on-non-financial-and-diversity-disclosure/ (Accessed June 18, 2019).

Guthrie, J., Ricceri, F., & Dumay, J. (2012). Reflections and projections: A decade of intellectual capital accounting research. *The British Accounting Review, 44*(2), 68–82. https://doi.org/10.1016/j.bar.2012.03.004.

Howitt, R., Thurm, R. (2018). From monocapitalism to multicapitalism: 21st century system value creation. Available at: https://blogs.thomsonreuters.com/sustainability/2018/06/07/executive-perspective-from-monocapitalism-to-multicapitalism-21st-century-system-value-creation/. Accessed 24 June 2019.

Institute of Directors in Southern Africa (IoDSA). (2016). Report on corporate governance for South Africa (King IV), Johannesburg. Available at: https://www.adams.africa/wp-content/uploads/2016/11/King-IV-Report.pdf (Accessed June 21, 2019).

International Integrated Reporting Council (IIRC). (2013). The international <IR > framework, international integrated reporting council, London. Available at: http://www.integratedreporting.org/wp-content/uploads/2015/03/13-12-08-THE-INTERNATIONAL-IR-FRAMEWORK-2-1.pdf. (Accessed September 16, 2019).

International Integrated Reporting Council (IIRC). (2014). Creating value to the board, international integrated reporting council, London. Available at: https://integratedreporting.org/wp-content/uploads/2015/04/Value-to-the-Board.pdf (Accessed August 17, 2019).

International Integrated Reporting Council (IIRC). (2017). Breaking through: IIRC 2017 integrated report, international integrated reporting council, London. Available at: https://integratedreporting.org/integratedreport2017/download_manager/index.html.

La Torre, M., Dumay, J., Rea, M. A., & Abhayawansa, S. (2019). A "Journey" toward a safe harbor: The rhetorical process of the international integrated reporting council. *The British Accounting Review*. https://doi.org/10.1016/j.bar.2019.100836.

Lee, K. W., & Yeo, G. H.-H. (2016). The association between integrated reporting and firm valuation. *Review of Quantitative Finance and Accounting, 47*(4), 1221–1250. https://doi.org/10.1007/s11156-015-0536-y.

Lounsboury, M. (2008). Institutional rationality and practice variation: New directions in the institutional analysis of practice. *Accounting, Organizations and Society, 33*(4–5), 349–361. https://doi.org/10.1016/j.aos.2007.04.001.

Merchant, K. A., & Van der Stede, W. (2007). *Management control systems: Performance measurement, evaluation, and incentives* (2nd ed.). New York: Prentice Hall.

Milne, M. J., & Gray, R. (2013). W(h)ither ecology? The triple bottom line, the global reporting initiative, and corporate sustainability reporting. *Journal of Business Ethics, 118*(1), 13–29. https://doi.org/10.1007/s10551-012-1543-8.

Monciardini, D., Dumay, J., Biondi, L. (2016). Integrated reporting and EU law. *Competing, converging or complementary regulatory frameworks?* Paper presented at the and EU Law. Competing, converging or complementary regulatory frameworks?—Life-cycle based management and reporting for sustainable business. 29–30 November 2016, Oslo, Norway.

Petty, R., & Guthrie, J. (2000). Intellectual capital literature review: Measurement, reporting and management. *Journal of Intellectual Capital, 1*(2), 155–176. https://doi.org/10.1108/14691930010348731.

Sabelfeld, S. and Dumay, J. (2018). *Adoption of integrated reporting: Lost in local translation?* Paper presented at the Financial Reporting Workshop, University of Bologna, 14–15 June 2018.

Stubbs, W., & Higgins, C. (2018). Stakeholders' perspectives on the role of regulatory reform in integrated reporting. *Journal of Business Ethics, 147*(3), 489–508. https://doi.org/10.1007/s10551-015-2954-0.

Suchman, M. C. (1995). Managing legitimacy: Strategic and institutional approaches. *The Academy of Management Review, 20*(3), 571–610. https://doi.org/10.2307/258788.

Thomson, I. (2015). 'But does sustainability need capitalism or an integrated report' a commentary on 'The International Integrated Reporting Council: A story of failure' by Flower. *J Critical Perspectives on Accounting, 27,* 18–22. https://doi.org/10.1016/j.cpa.2014.07.003.

United Nations Conference on Trade and Development (UNCTAD). (2019). Guidance on core indicators for entity reporting on contribution towards implementation of the sustainable development goals, United Nations, New York. Available at: https://unctad.org/en/pages/PublicationWebflyer.aspx?publicationid=2469 (Accessed September 14, 2019).

Zhou, S., Simnett, R., & Green, W. (2017). Does integrated reporting matter to the capital market? *Abacus, 53*(1), 94–132. https://doi.org/10.1111/abac.12104.

The manufacturer's authorised representative in the EU is Springer
Nature Customer Service Centre GmbH, Europaplatz 3, 69115 Heidelberg,
Germany. If you have any concerns regarding our products, please
contact ProductSafety@springernature.com

Printed and bound by CPI Group (UK) Ltd, Croydon, CR0 4YY
05/10/2026
02228151-0004